Introduction

New mums think that new dads are useless. Do they have a point? Well, as we're talking in generalisations here, the answer to that question is also going to be 'yes', but it's not an insoluble problem.

We have to accept that women are naturally going to be the main care providers. They are biologically tuned-in to that role and the female body offers everything that a newborn baby needs in order to survive. But this puts a lot of pressure on mums and can cause problems for both parents. A mum needs help but will feel that she is the only person able to do the job properly; a dad may feel excluded and can become 'useless'.

A new dad must signal his intention to be fully involved with the care of his child as early as possible, and then start living up to that promise as soon as his baby is born. Both partners need to be clear that the responsibilities for the baby and household are going to be shared equally, wherever possible.

A new mum will always believe that she can do things quicker for the baby than anyone else (she's probably right), and will often refuse help even when she is desperate and you are offering. It's stressful, she'll say, and there's no time to show you what to do. But this means that not only are you pushed to the sidelines but you don't have the chance to learn so that you can take over next time. So you not only need to be assertive to carve out a role for yourself, you also need to know what you are doing and be confident about it so that you clearly have something to offer.

Most fathers learn babycare through trial and error, trial and error, trial and error. What this book aims to do is give you a shortcut to the wisdom of experienced dads who have learned the hard way.

Some of the advice will work for you immediately, other ideas will work one day but not the next. Some advice you will simply scoff at and turn the page – it may seem crazy or just not relevant to your everyday life. That's fine because there are no rules for bringing up babies; every child is different. But sometimes the most unlikely ideas will work when you least expect it, so it's good to try different approaches just in case they surprise you.

There are chapters on all the basic techniques plus some big ideas to get your head around, such as how to handle the responsibility of being a role model. You will quickly learn what has to be done and how to do it. All you need then is practice. And you can tailor your approach in discussion with your partner to meet her needs and of your child.

In short, this book should give you everything you need to make yourself useful. Good luck!

That's my baby

How your baby might look

Boy? Girl? Alien? All babies look a little like ET, with or without a healthy head of hair. It may help to think what you would look like had you spent nine months confined in a hot bath, before being forced out through the plughole – raw, shrivelled, swollen and bruised are the first words that spring to mind. Of course, your baby may be beautiful from the start. But if you think not, other adoring family members will soon convince you that your baby is exceptionally handsome!

GET YOUR PRIORITIES RIGHT

The first few hours after the birth are all about relief and recovery. Your baby has to be gently settled into his new world, your partner badly needs a rest and you will be feeling somewhat shell-shocked. There will be practical things for you to organise but stick to the immediate needs of your new family, rather than rushing around trying to find 'something to do'. What your partner will appreciate most is you giving full attention to her and the baby; seeing and hearing how much you love them. At a really basic level, your 'acceptance' of the baby is vital to start the family relationship off on the right foot. Your partner needs to feel that she and the baby have your unconditional support for the years ahead, so start as you mean to go on, and spend time telling her how you feel and listening to how she feels.

Head Your baby's skull may be squashed into a slightly pointed shape. This can happen during a normal vaginal delivery and even in some Caesarean births. In both cases, your baby has spent time upside down in the birth canal. Don't worry; this gradually evens out. Babies born with the use of forceps or ventouse suction may have bruising.

Fontanelles There will be two soft, pulsating patches on your baby's skull that allow it the flexibility to be squeezed through the birth canal. The fontanelles do not knit together fully for about two years but they are covered by a tough membrane.

Hair Your baby may have a full head of hair or none at all. Whatever hair he does have will soon be replaced by new growth, which may be of a different colour and texture.

Ears Some edges of the ears may be folded over at birth but they will gradually return to their natural shape.

Eyes These may be bloodshot or puffy and only one may be opened at a time. Most Caucasian babies start with dark blue eyes, while most African and Asian babies have dark grey or brown eyes at birth. Their true colour will not appear for about six months.

Nose This may be flattened.

Mouth Very rarely, a baby will have an early tooth that will need to be removed.

Skin The appearance of your baby's skin will differ depending on whether he arrived early, on time or late. Two things you may notice are lanugo – fine downy hair, and vernix – a white protective grease that covers the skin. The longer your baby spends in the womb, the less likely he is to have these at birth.

Chest Nipples may be swollen and giving off a discharge due to the action of hormones. Any swelling or discharge will disappear in a few days.

Umbilical cord The stump of the umbilical cord will be clamped to prevent bleeding. It will soon dry out, turn black and eventually fall off.

Genitals These are often swollen at first, following a large dose of hormones from the mother before birth.

Fingers The fingers and nails are perfectly formed at birth. The nails can be sharp and are sometimes blue. Any blueness should resolve in a few days.

Posture Your baby's knees will be drawn up close to his body.

Feet Perfectly formed at birth, the feet and toes look delicate but can be very flexible.

Mike's story

When my daughter was born she looked so battered and bruised. It had been a long, hard birth, involving forceps. She was such a tiny little thing; I was amazed how tough she must have been to come through all that. The imprint of the forceps was clearly visible on her head and her skin looked very raw. It was a traumatic experience for all of us, but within a few weeks the marks had disappeared and we could see just how beautiful she really was.

What your baby needs

Once your baby is born, you need to know how she 'works' so that you can ensure that all of her needs are being met. Actually, these boil down to a concise shortlist of three: food, sleep and human contact. She also needs her nappy changed between six and 12 times a day, but you probably knew that already.

No doubt your partner will provide for these needs most of the time, especially if she's breastfeeding, but if you understand what's going on with your baby, you can step in to help whenever the opportunity arises. Your partner will feel reassured that you are taking an interest and trying to develop your babycare skills. And every minute that you get to interact with your baby, is a chance to build the relationship between you. You will know when your baby needs any of the three essentials because she will instruct you through the age-old medium of crying.

Feeding
The average baby is said to enjoy around 12 'meals' a day, as she settles into a period of rapid growth after leaving the womb. Actually, in the first few days after the birth, your baby's weight will probably drop by about 10 per cent, but she will put it all back on over the next couple of weeks. Her weight will then increase quickly over the first year, often by as much as half a kilo (or 1 pound) per week.

Your baby can live exclusively on milk for at least the first six months, before gradually being weaned onto solid foods. Breast and formula milk both contain everything your baby needs to develop properly, although only breast milk contains the natural ingredients that will enhance her immune system.

Sleep
Babies need a lot of sleep. And unless your baby has a problem such as colic, which can cause her to cry for hours, you will probably wonder what all the fuss over sleepless nights is about. Indeed, if you're lucky, your paternity leave can be a very quiet time.

Your baby is doing a huge amount of growing; she's had a traumatic birth experience;

15 The number of hours that the average baby will sleep each day in the first three months of her life.

and she's learning a whole new way of living. No wonder she's tired! However, your baby is unlikely to sleep for long periods and will probably wake up every three to four hours, day and night – that's the difficult part.

Gradually, the amount of sleep she requires will lessen, but she will still need about 12 hours a night at the age of three. The challenge for you and your partner will be to educate her in good sleeping habits to ensure that by that age she's not still waking you up during the night.

100 The amount of excrement, in kilograms, that the average baby excretes in her first 2½ years of life (plus about 250 litres of urine).

Human contact
There have been many studies that show the importance of human contact to the healthy mental and physical development of babies. We all feel better for a hug – and your baby is no

8 The average weight in kilograms that you lift when carrying a six-month-old boy. At 18 months, the average weight is 12 kilograms.

different. Unhappy at being pulled out of her cosy womb, she'll need all the reassurance and comforting she can get to make her feel happy in the outside world. You may feel that she

should start to develop a sense of independence as soon as possible, but leaving her to cry at a young age will simply make her feel that she's on her own in the world and nobody loves her. On the other hand, carrying and holding her will help her to feel emotionally secure. Indeed, you may be amazed at how much carrying your baby expects in the first six months, as she tries to recreate the feelings of security and motion that she experienced while in the womb.

Survival instincts

Your baby will exhibit a range of reflexes during the first six months of life, all of which are linked to achieving her basic needs – in effect, a series of deep-seated survival instincts that have been part of the human make-up since the very beginning.

The sucking reflex. Your baby's natural instinct is to suck whatever is put into her mouth – her mum's breast, a bottle-teat, or your finger. It's a crucial survival instinct and a strong suck is a sign of a healthy baby. She may also suck her thumb or finger to soothe herself.

The rooting reflex. Tickle the side of your baby's cheek and she will turn towards you and try to suck on your finger; this helps her find food. Tickle your baby's lips to encourage her to feed. This reflex continues while your baby nurses.

The grasping reflex. If you place your finger in your baby's hand she will grasp it tightly. Her grasp can be so strong that you can almost lift her up by her arms. This reflex usually disappears after about four months.

The startle reflex. When your baby hears a loud noise or is moved suddenly, her hands will shoot out to her sides, fingers spread out. Then she'll bring her arms back to her chest, fists tightly clenched and probably end with a crying episode.

The walking or stepping reflex. If you hold your baby upright under her arms and let her feet touch a flat surface, she will naturally make stepping movements and try to move forward. This reflex usually disappears by the time your baby is two months old.

The diving reflex. Although you should never leave your baby to swim under water, if you place your newborn under the surface for a short time she'll swim happily because her lungs automatically seal off under water.

What your baby can do

For the first six weeks of a baby's life his main objective is to acclimatise himself to the very different world outside the womb. He has spent nine months floating in an environment that caters for his every need – now he has to cry for his supper, and for everything else. So it's a terrible shock to him at first.

As he becomes more comfortable, he will begin to explore his body and its new environment. With your help, he will develop so quickly, both mentally and physically, that sometimes you will notice daily changes.

Generally, the bigger developments tend to happen in spurts. Your baby will appear to be on the verge of a change for a while, almost storing up information as if he knows he is about to take a leap into the unknown. Then he takes that leap and starts doing things that you would never have thought possible the day before. But all children are different and develop skills at a different pace, and any general guidelines can only be taken as such. Some babies will walk at about 10 months but may take longer than normal to develop language skills, whereas others

WEEK 4
He may look around to find source of sound. Watches alertly when fed and talked to. Stops crying when picked up and talked to. When lying on his stomach, may pick up his head for a minute.

WEEK 6
Your baby begins to recognise you and smiles at you, even if you are not talking to him. When you smile and talk at the same time, he may smile back and gurgle.

WEEK 8
He may look at his hands, opening them up, grasping one with the other and twiddling his fingers. He can also focus on and follow a toy placed about 20 cm in front of his face. This is an important phase for learning the connection between what he can see, hear and touch.

WEEK 10
Beginning to take an interest in what goes on around her. She is awake for longer periods.

MONTH 3
Will look up when being fed. Starts to anticipate enjoyable things – gets excited when sees bottle prepared, for example.

MONTH 4
Exhibits curiosity at new things and puts them in his mouth. He will enjoy bouncing on his feet while you hold him upright. He may begin to pull up his knees and push with his feet, and raise his shoulders to push with his hands, using muscles that he will later need for crawling. He can focus over a wide visual range and can shape his hands to hold things easily. He may start to cry when you leave the room.

MONTH 5
The muscles in his back have strengthened and he can sit comfortably, provided he has some support at the base of his spine. He can also turn his head from side to side.

MONTH 6
He may become excited when he hears the voice of someone he knows well. He laughs and chuckles and starts using his hands to explore different textures. Reaches with one or both hands to get hold of a toy. Can lift head, chest and abdomen off the floor when lying on his stomach.

will confidently babble at 18 months but will not walk until they are nearly two years old.

This uncertainty is partly what makes your own baby's development so fascinating to watch, and the first year will probably be one of the most exciting times of your life. So aim to be involved as much as possible and try not to miss the first smiles, crawls, steps and 'words' – all the things that will become etched in to your memory forever.

WE NEED TO TALK | ABOUT KEEPING UP WITH CHANGES

Having to go back to work comes as a real shock to the system and you will wonder how you can keep up with your child's development when you spend so much time out of the home. Your partner is totally engrossed in caring for your baby 24 hours a day, and she may not always recognise the changes that would be significant to you. Tell your partner how interested you are in all the small things of her daily life and encourage her to start keeping a simple journal. This is something that many mums say they wish they had done, but there just never seemed time. It would help you keep in touch, help her to express her feelings and work out stresses and, of course, provide a wonderful record of the period to look back on in the future.

MONTH 7
He starts to use his fingers and thumbs for grasping and holding. He may repeat one-syllable words to make two syllables, for example, 'ma-ma', 'da-da'. Starts to use spoon. Will probably be able to support himself in the crawling position with only one hand.

MONTH 8
He may sit for long periods without support and lean over to pick up things. He can push up onto all-fours and make a variety of rolling, pushing and turning movements. He starts to crawl or may prefer to shuffle across the floor on his tummy or bottom.

MONTH 9
He may pull himself up using furniture for support. He can crawl or bottom-shuffle. He may find it easier to crawl backwards at first. May recognise his own name. Plays peek-a-boo. Will enjoy self-feeding with finger foods. He can point at objects, clap and wave goodbye.

MONTH 10
He can take his whole weight when held in a standing position but cannot yet balance. He can uncurl his fingers to release an object and enjoys dropping anything he picks up. Will stop doing something when he hears the word, 'No'.

MONTH 11
He starts to pull himself up to a standing position and may get stuck standing up. May take sideways steps around furniture.

MONTH 12
He starts to stand alone and may take a few steps herself. He can pick up tiny objects, and enjoys throwing things and filling and emptying containers. He may say his first real word, identifying an object or a person. May give you a toy or other object if asked. He listens and points to a familiar item in a storybook. He returns affectionate hugs with his own cuddles.

How you can relate to each other

In the first few hours of your baby's life, there's a very good chance that she will hear you speak and turn towards you. She cannot see you properly yet, but she recognises your voice. You are her father for much of the time that she was in her mother's womb, she could hear sounds coming from outside of her body. One of those she heard most often was your voice. You were already part of her life and environment before she was born. The relationship is already established and now it's up to you to build on that strong start.

You will probably feel a little awkward at first, because you do not have an obvious role other than continuing to support your partner as you did during the pregnancy and birth. Your baby, meanwhile, seems purely interested in being fed by her mother, so what can you do to build the relationship?

As I said, your baby may well recognise your voice from the womb. At that stage, her hearing was more attuned to lower frequencies, so your deeper voice should have been more audible – except that she was inside her mother's body, so her voice came across more directly, despite her lighter tone. The situation is similar now that she's outside the womb. In the early weeks and months she will know that you are with her but her most direct relationship will be with her mother, whom she is programmed to latch onto in order to survive.

So, in order for you, as a new dad, to make the most of the limited opportunities you have to develop a rapport with your baby, it's important that you understand the ways in which your baby relates to you.

- Getting up close is key. Your new baby can only see about 20 cm in front of her, so give her the best view that you possibly can. In fact, it's been shown that babies can imitate their father's facial expressions within an hour of being born. This not only tells us that new babies are more developed than we think, but also should encourage dads to make an extra effort to communicate.

- Her sense of touch is still developing but your stubbly face will definitely feel different to her mother's – you just have to be careful not to graze her sensitive skin.

- As for smell, she has been able to do that since she was lounging around in the womb, but she will not recognise you by scent in the way that she knows her mummy. Holding her close will help her to store your smell in her memory.

- Carrying her around with you and gently rocking her, is a great way to meet all of these bonding needs at the same time, and the motion also helps to develop her sense of balance.

- Talking is also very important. She will love listening to you speak and sing as you cuddle her. Once you're able to start feeding her, this will create the perfect mix of attention from daddy. Until then, give her your little finger to suck on when she needs reassurance.

2

Suddenly, I'm a Dad!

Emotional reactions

How are you feeling? This is a question not often asked of dads in the first weeks after the birth. If it is, a proper answer is not really expected – it's more of a joke than a genuine inquiry as to the father's well-being. After all, it's the mother who has had months of discomfort, an agonising birth experience, and months of exhaustion yet to come. But men's health is now a hot topic, and there is an increasing amount of research being done in this area.

Just as being at the birth forces you to experience a wide range of emotions, the weeks following that experience can be equally as tough. The excitement of the build-up to the event and the initial high of holding your own child, can quickly deteriorate into self-doubt, resentment and fear for the future, as the reality of the situation kicks in.

On top of all your new responsibilities, you have less time, money and energy. You may feel guilty if you did not attend the birth, or if you were there, that you put your partner through such a painful experience. If it was a difficult birth and you had to put on a gown and rush into the operating theatre with the doctors and nurses, you could be in shock for days afterwards. Some men are unhappy with the gender of their baby, because they really wanted a child of the other sex; others are perfectly happy but worry that they do not feel the intense love for their babies that they imagine should occur instantaneously.

So there are all sorts of emotional reactions that come in to play.

But you are a man, and the stereotypical role of the man is to be strong, silent and able to cope. You're allowed a few tears at the birth but after that you just have to get on with it. That's what family and friends will expect from you, and perhaps even your partner will feel the same, believing you a failure if you don't live up to the stereotype.

Luckily, the vast majority of men manage to get through the first few wobbly weeks and push on to fully enjoy the baby experience. And the best way to ensure that you banish any baby blues, is to get involved with your baby's care. You have to accept that this new addition to your life is going to be the centre of attention – permanently. Once you relax with that idea and get as much hands-on experience of your baby as possible, your self-esteem will return as your confidence grows, and you'll soon start to feel

MALE POST-NATAL DEPRESSION

Post-natal depression has long been thought of as a condition that only affects mums but researchers are now starting to take it seriously as an issue for dads. A recent study of more than 8,000 fathers in the UK found that eight weeks after the birth, one in 25 was suffering post-natal depression, compared to one in 10 mothers. Of course, just about everyone will experience a few rough weeks, but if the feelings continue, then real depression can be a devastating blow for the family, to the point where a parent leaves the home or becomes suicidal. It's also been suggested that depression in new fathers has particularly bad effects on the development of their sons, who appear to be influenced from a very early age by the behaviour of their fathers.

The big problem for men is that they are much less likely than women to ask for help. But depression is not something to be ashamed of, and a simple course of treatment is usually all that's required.

the love coming back to you in hugs, kisses and smiles.

Reordering your priorities

Responsibility is the thing that comes along just after your baby arrives in the delivery room. If you haven't felt it before, you certainly will when the umbilical cord is cut. Your baby is out in the world now, and your partner is no longer totally responsible for her well-being. He's your baby and your responsibility for at least the next 18 years. It's a big new feeling that some dads find very difficult to handle.

There are basically two ways of approaching responsibility. You can accept it grudgingly and allow yourself to be pushed and pulled around by it, or you can take it on board with a positive, proactive attitude, that makes you, and those around you, feel good.

If you select option one, and muddle along trying to keep your life exactly as it was before, then you'll be spending a lot of time asking yourself why you wanted to have a child in the first place. It's only by selecting option two, the positive, proactive approach to fatherhood, that you'll actually find out the answer.

Inevitably, a more family-oriented lifestyle is going to mean less time for non-family activities, such as nights out after work, one-to-one time with your partner, and even the simple pleasure of lounging around on Sunday morning reading the newspapers.

In short, having a baby is the time when you are finally forced to grow up. And if you haven't done so already, you need to re-order your priorities. What are the really important

WE NEED TO TALK | ABOUT FEELING DEPRESSED

Real depression can be difficult to recognise in the turbulent months after childbirth, and health professionals are not trained to look for the signs in fathers. If you experience a loss of interest in your usual activities, difficulty concentrating or making decisions, feelings of worthlessness or guilt, changes in appetite or sleep and excessive anxiety about your baby's health, then it's possible that you could be depressed.

The best thing you can do at this stage is talk to your partner, or a friend or health professional – at which point you are already beginning to solve the problem. Bear in mind that, as a man, you are more likely to suffer from depression if you are unemployed, you have previously been depressed, or your partner has suffered from depression.

things in your life? Not just now but in the future as well? This may be the first time that you have looked more than just a few months or years ahead. As morbid as it sounds, the one thing you must do is write a will.

While you're starting to get your head around all of these big life issues, you'll also need to review your finances. Babies do not come cheap. There are all the essential one-off items to buy, such as the pushchair, cot and car seat, plus daily consumables such as nappies, clothes and possibly formula milk and bottles. And the list keeps growing as your baby does. If you have not already moved home to accommodate your new family member, then no doubt you'll soon be looking for a place with more space.

This may be the first time that you and your partner have really tackled financial issues together, working as a real partnership, but this is an area where you can take a lead and ensure that this is one thing your partner does not have to worry about.

Ideally, you would have started discussing financial matters before your baby was born, when you had more time and fewer distractions. But these issues are easily put off at the best of times. Now you have the baby, you can see the importance of rearranging your family finances, but your partner is immersed in the day-to-day care and may be less able to see the bigger picture. You need to take the lead on this, so agree a good time to sit down together and discuss the situation. Don't try to sort out too many things in the first meeting, just focus on the immediate issues and ensure that decisions are made. Do as much preparation as possible beforehand to make the choices as straightforward as they can be, but take care to ensure that your partner has an equal say in the proceedings.

Looking after yourself

There is nothing crazy about a new dad spending all day in his pyjamas. When you are on paternity leave, all social norms are suspended. If friends, neighbours or relatives call unannounced, just to see how you are, the most they can reasonably expect is to see a pale face appear at the window. Give them the best smile you can muster and a thumbs up. If they don't get the message, open the curtains wider to reveal your crumpled pyjamas. If that still doesn't see them off, call the police.

The point is that with so much going on with your baby and your partner, it's really difficult to remember to look after yourself. But they need you to be strong enough, both mentally and physically, to support them. So forget about other people's expectations and concentrate on the three of you. Try to relax as much as possible – even taking the occasional nap – and don't feel you have to do anything that is not essential for the well-being of your new family unit.

Eating well is something that you really need to keep up. While good nutrition is essential for your partner, particularly if she's breastfeeding, you also need to keep up your vitamin levels to help cope with sleep deprivation and all the extra chores. And your baby will soon be attracting all the local viruses so you need your immune system to be strong.

Try to learn a few simple recipes for healthy comfort food, rather than relying on takeaways and TV dinners. Good food can feel like a life-saver at times likes this, and the preparation can be a great relaxation technique. Your partner also will appreciate some home cooking.

Jake's story

While I was on paternity leave, often the only reason I would get dressed during the day was to go out to the shops in the middle of the afternoon. As well as picking up any essentials, I would always buy cream cakes for a tea-time treat, which never failed to raise our spirits and energy levels. I would also look out for a surprise for my wife, just something small such as nice soap, a magazine, a video or a favourite food she hadn't been able to eat during pregnancy. That always went down well.

Cutting out bad habits

There are two very good reasons for reviewing your personal behaviour, ideally before your baby even arrives. Firstly, you will soon realise that your baby copies everything that you do. Virtually all of a baby's behaviour comes from observing other humans, and your child naturally will see you as the star of the show.

The other reason is that many of the classic human vices are going to have an impact on your baby's health, whether it becomes obvious now or only later in life. Smoking is the number one issue.

As far as your own well-being is concerned, if you're a smoker, the biggest single thing you can do to improve your health is to stop smoking. If you find it impossible to give up, then at least don't smoke in the house. The fumes can contribute to cot death, and generally your baby will suffer from more childhood illnesses, such as ear infections, than the children of non-smokers. Your baby also will be more likely to smoke as an adult. In short, there will probably never be a time in your life when you have more good reasons to stop being a slave to the tobacco companies.

On the other hand, a moderate amount of alcohol will probably be one of the things that keeps you going as the parent of a young baby – the thought of relaxing with a cold beer or glass of wine at the end of the day can be a great incentive. Indeed, there is a lot of medical evidence to show that the relaxing properties of alcohol can help counter the destructive effects of stress on the body. But don't fall into the trap of thinking that alcohol helps you sleep – it might make you feel tired but the quality of sleep will not be as good. The key is to drink in moderation, and don't allow yourself to become reliant on alcohol, or other drugs, in order to get through the day. Instead, try learning some relaxation techniques that do the same job without the hangover.

Swearing is something that many of us do without even thinking, which can make it very difficult to give up. You and your partner will really have to police each other's speech, because this is a time of great temptation! In one sense, swearing is a good way of releasing

HOW MUCH DOES A BABY COST?

Parents in the UK are said to spend more on bringing up their children than any other country in Europe, topping £46,000 in the first five years of a child's life. From birth to age 21, UK parents spend approximately £140,000 on each child. Meanwhile, in America, The US Department of Agriculture estimates that a family with an annual income of $70,000 will spend about $270,000 in the first 17 years of a child's life.

any anger or frustration. You just have to make sure that you are not within earshot of your baby, because you will never know, until it's too late, when he has started retaining some of your favourite phrases to unleash on unsuspecting visitors. So, if you can start to moderate your behaviour early on, you'll have fewer problems when your baby is transformed into the more formidable shape of a toddler.

You may not think it's so important when you baby is only a few days old, but the sooner you get to grips with any habits that you don't want your child to emulate, the better. You don't have any bad habits? Ask your partner. She'll have a comprehensive list.

The effects on your relationship

As you now know, the man's role in pregnancy and birth is essentially one of support. Put like that, it doesn't sound much, but ask any mother and she'll remind you just how important it was to have the strong support of a partner during one of the most challenging experiences of her life. And much the same is true in the months following the birth.

Some men say that they over-prepared for the actual event and then, once the momentous day had passed, they felt totally unprepared for the long-term commitment that followed.

Having worked through the emotional stresses and strains of deciding to have a baby, and then actually doing it, you probably feel pretty good that your relationship has survived this far! But beware, the first year after the birth will undoubtedly push your relationship to the limits. Just the lack of sleep will be damaging to your everyday relationship, let alone all the other challenges you will face as a couple.

This is when the traditional failing of men – lack of communication – can become a major problem. It may be difficult at first, but the solution to this one is to discuss issues early. If you came through the stresses of pregnancy and birth with your relationship still feeling strong – if not strengthened – then obviously that will stand you in good stead. If there were problems that were not addressed, then you will need to do so soon to prevent them festering.

In order to head off problems, you need to be constantly aware of your partner's emotional needs. Be prepared to listen to her talk about her day, how she's feeling, and the problems she's facing, without trying to offer instant solutions. She will often just want to unburden herself, and your attempts to wave a magic wand will suggest to her that you really don't understand what she's going through.

She will also want to see and hear you being positive about the baby. Take a step

WE NEED TO TALK | ABOUT GOOD HABITS

When it comes to cutting down drinking and smoking, your partner should have a headstart because she's already faced those challenges over nine months of pregnancy. But the relief of finally giving birth may mean that she feels like throwing herself back in to cigarettes and alcohol as a reward for her abstinence! The stresses of caring for the baby can also make these very attractive ways of trying to relax at the end of the day. So keeping control of bad habits is going to be difficult for you both. You need to be open and honest, and support each other. If you start to feel uncomfortable about the amount your partner is drinking, but are unsure about how to approach the subject, one way to raise the issue without making 'accusations' is by telling her that you are going to cut down your own drinking. If you can set an example, sticking to your own guidelines, the chances are that your partner will follow.

back and look at the ways in which you speak and behave, and try to imagine how they might appear to someone who is feeling hyper-sensitive and looking out for signs of encouragement from her partner.

Inevitably, you are going to be relegated to the number two spot in her affections as she focuses on the needs of your baby, and there is really no way around this. 'Go away and do something useful' is a phrase you will soon get used to hearing. You just have to accept your supporting role at this part of the proceedings but do everything you can to be involved.

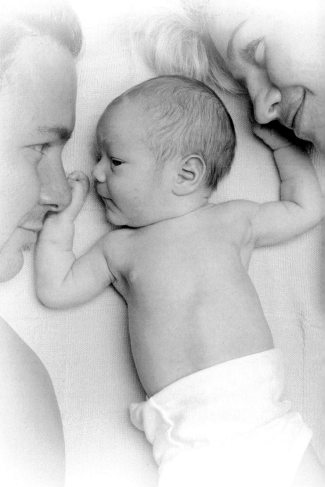

WE NEED TO TALK | ABOUT COMMUNICATING

When you are at work all day and your partner is at home with the baby, it may seem that you are inhabiting two totally separate worlds, making communication even more difficult than usual. Try to set a pattern for discussing things with your partner – work out the best times to raise issues, for example when you are both least tired, when you do not have the pressure of another chore coming up, and when you have both had a break from the baby to clear your minds. The essential point is to keep open the lines of communication. Finding time to talk is the first hurdle, and then you both have to feel like it when you finally sit down together.

Your sex life

The issue of sex will undoubtedly come up once the effects of the birth experience start to wear off, and will provide another point of tension within your relationship. Neither of you may actually feel like sex – having got out of the habit during pregnancy, you are now simply too tired to do anything other than sleep when in bed together.

Generally, your partner's self-confidence will have been affected by her changing appearance and new home-based role, and you will need to be positive to build up her self-esteem so that she actually comes to feel attractive again. But you also may have to resign yourself to the fact that this part of your relationship may never be the same again, in that sex just will not happen as regularly as before. The upside could be that abstinence makes the heart grow fonder, and when sex does happen, it's worth the wait. Just remember to be prepared, because although your partner is not immediately fertile after giving birth, by the time her first period arrives she will have been fertile for about two weeks.

Charlie's story

Before our daughter arrived, we used to go out to restaurants a lot and really dress up and have a good time. But once she was born, we couldn't bear to leave her with a babysitter so we rarely had a night out together. Instead, we decided to make Saturday nights special at home. We would always make a big effort to dress up, cook a really good, but simple, meal, buy some quality wine, set the table and light a few candles. It gave us something to look forward to each week and helped keep alive the romance in our relationship.

Usually you will be advised to wait six weeks after the birth before resuming intercourse, and you will probably have to change your method of contraception because oral contraceptives do not mix well with breastfeeding.

What the lack of sex does mean is that one of the main physical connection points in your relationship will be missing. A feeling of closeness is probably the most difficult and the most important part of the relationship to maintain, so you will need to compensate with lots of cuddling and kind words to keep your partner feeling loved and appreciated. It may sound cheesy, but women will tell you that 'regular cuddles' are absolutely vital in keeping their spirits up, and you will probably find that it does the same for you.

POST-NATAL DEPRESSION

The 'baby blues' affects about half of all new mums, starting between three and five days after delivery, and is thought to be linked to changes in hormone levels, exacerbated by exhaustion and sleep deprivation. More serious depression affects about 10 per cent of mums in the first six months. This can be very destructive to family relationships, especially as the symptoms (see box page 15) will be difficult for the father to separate from what he might expect in the circumstances, or he may simply find depression difficult to comprehend. If you are concerned about your partner, speak to a health professional.

Seeing your partner in a new light

No doubt you will have already developed new insights into your partner's character through the pregnancy and birth of your child. She may have become a very different person to you, as you watched her body transform into the child-bearing shape, and saw her courage as she coped with the trials of childbirth. You should be extremely proud of her.

Most of the physical changes will now reverse but, depending on the nature of the birth, in some ways she will never be the same again. Mentally, she will definitely be going through a major transformation as she reassesses her future in the light of motherhood, because you can never predict how you will feel as a parent until you have your baby in your arms.

On the other hand, these changes will lead some men to see their partners in a harsh new light. Some will feel that they have lost the person they once loved. They didn't know their partners as well as they thought they did, and perhaps now they have seen too much. They may have been put out by a partner's changing shape, her lack of interest in sex, and the restrictions that the pregnancy placed on their lifestyles. They may no longer feel physically attracted because of what they have seen in the months leading up to the birth and in the delivery room. Now her absorption with the baby further heightens the disappointment.

Many of these feelings are just temporary, and if you find yourself reacting in this way, bear in mind that things will even out as you gradually get over the shock of the birth and life returns, almost, to normal. But if problems persist, and you don't feel able to discuss them with your partner, seek the advice of a close friend or health professional, who can at least help you put the issues into perspective.

What does it mean to be a mum?
The physical and mental challenges that you both face in the early months of parenthood may well obscure the more fundamental shift that your partner is going through. Whether she likes it or not, she is experiencing a major change of identity, especially if the plan is for her to become a full-time carer.

■ **TOP TIPS The perfect partner**
If you are aiming to be a great partner, there are some things that new mums will definitely be looking for in new dads. If you can measure up to this list, then you are well on the way to perfection … until she writes her next list.
- Change nappies.
- Get up in the night to tend to your baby.
- Share the housework equally.
- Tidy up the bathroom after using it.
- Notice when essential items are running out and replace them.
- Cook a delicious meal quickly and clean up afterwards.
- Spend as much time as necessary comforting your crying baby.
- Be sensitive, understanding and tender.
- Take it for granted that you should be doing these things.

How ever your partner saw herself before, now her only identity is that of 'mother'. You still have the prestigious role of 'provider', as well as the glossy new 'father' identity. If you fail at fatherhood, at least you have your work to bolster your self-esteem, and vice versa. But a full-time mum who feels that she is failing at motherhood has no other identity to fall back on. When things aren't going well at home, she cannot just head off to the office to feel valued and fulfilled. So you need to be vigilant to ensure that she's experiencing those feelings within her role as a mother, while at the same time allowing her opportunities to escape, socialise and do things for herself.

Mums who continue to work outside the home may be tackling similar issues as they struggle to cope with the conflicting demands of motherhood and work, and feeling guilty that they cannot give their best attention to either. Others will just be glad to get out of the house, spend time with some adults, and return refreshed, even though organising this double life is often difficult and stressful.

Valuing your partner

An important part of supporting your partner is vocalising your feelings for her. Helping her in practical ways, such as doing the washing up, is something that should happen as a matter of course, so don't expect too much credit for that. But what she needs to hear you say, regularly and meaningfully, is what a wonderful job she is doing, how proud you are of the way she is bringing up your child, and how much you love her. Kisses and cuddles are vital to keep her spirits up. In short, do everything you can to make her feel like a valued individual, as opposed to a babycare machine. These may seem like minor points, but if you don't pay attention to the fine detail of your relationship, there will be trouble ahead.

■ **TOP TIPS What not to say …**

The one question that you should never ask a new mum is 'When are you going back to work?'. It may seem an innocent enough inquiry but the clear inference is that nurturing future generations – for free – is not real work. If you ask this question to a full-time mum, it's highly likely that she will produce an axe from the shopping basket under her pushchair and chop off your legs at the knees. Your head will then be at the perfect height for a second swing of the axe to lop it off. You won't ask that question again. And rightly so.

A NECESSARY EXPENSE

What do you do when you come home from work to find that your partner is wearing yet another new item of clothing? Doesn't she realise that the family finances are stretched on a single income? This is a difficult situation for dads, because it seems so obviously wrong to be buying clothes when money is tight.
But many mums feel that they have sacrificed their individuality by devoting so much of their time to children and the family. Clothes make her feel good, boost her confidence and help to re-assert her identity as an individual. So as long as she's not spending outrageous amounts, there can be important benefits to the family. Think of it as a legitimate 'business expense' in her role as a mother. And be sure to tell her how good she looks!

3

How do I bond with my baby?

Getting up close and personal

One of the first things you will see in the delivery room after your partner gives birth, is your new baby being placed on her mother's chest for a first cuddle. This is raw bonding in its most basic form and most experts feel that you need to start bonding with your baby, both physically and mentally, as soon as possible after her birth.

Positive attitude

Your partner will inevitably have a head start on forming a loving connection with your new child – after all, she has been carrying the baby around inside her body for the past nine months. But not all mums feel that way immediately – and it's always going to be harder for the father. So don't be downhearted if you don't suddenly experience a rush of love for your baby; you will have plenty of time to get to know her and create a proper bond. During the early weeks particularly, you may find it

difficult to get close because your baby is almost totally dependent on your partner, but take the opportunity to spend time with her whenever you can. Make sure you prise her away from your partner to try some skin-to-skin bonding yourself – for example, giving her a bare-chested hug before dressing her after a nappy change.

The important thing for you, as with so much of the baby experience, is to approach the challenge with a positive attitude. Do that, and the bonding is bound to follow.

Communication

It's sometimes easy to forget that communication is about much more than simply talking. In fact, speech is believed to make up only about a third of communication between humans – the rest is non-verbal, or body language. Your baby cannot talk, but even within an hour of her birth she is able to

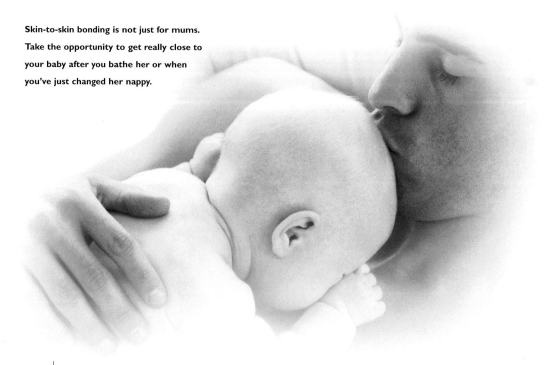

Skin-to-skin bonding is not just for mums. Take the opportunity to get really close to your baby after you bathe her or when you've just changed her nappy.

communicate with you and her mother. Try pulling faces at her and poking out your tongue, because there's a very good chance that she will copy you.

At the same time, talking is vital to her development, so chat to her as much as possible, even though you know she cannot understand you yet. And help her to visualise the pair of you together by holding her up to a mirror. She'll be fascinated by the image and you'll also find that it reinforces your growing feelings towards her.

Like any new relationship, the more you interact, the quicker you will feel comfortable with each other, the better you will understand each other's needs, and the sooner you will develop a mutual attachment.

Physical contact

The sooner that your baby gets to know you, and your smell, the sooner she will feel comforted in your presence, when she hears your voice or you pick her up. Give her lots of kisses and cuddles, stroking and massaging her skin whenever you get the chance. Let her fall asleep on you, sit her up next to you with your arm around her, and generally make her feel that she's your best friend.

Sharing the care

While there are lots of specific things that you can do to help along the bonding process, such as playing and massaging your baby, you can also build quality time into everyday routines. It's important that you support your partner as much as possible with the

PEEK-A-BOO

This game is fun for both parent and baby. Use exaggerated facial and vocal expressions as you cover your face and reveal it again to your baby. Even though you've 'disappeared' only momentarily, your baby will be happy to welcome you back.

WE NEED TO TALK | ABOUT SHARED CARE

Some new mothers find it difficult to share babycare. They may feel they are better at caring for the baby and that only the best is good enough. If your partner seems reluctant to let you help with feeding, dressing or bathing, you need to explain that her health, both mental and physical, is going to suffer unless she takes a break – and that's not good for the baby. Tell her that you need some quality time with your baby on a regular basis. If your partner feels your babycare skills are not up to scratch, tell her you can only improve if you are allowed to practice. To help generate a sense of teamwork, make sure to ask your partner to show you exactly how she does everything, and ask for feedback afterwards.

BABY MASSAGE

Fathers don't experience the nine months of physical closeness that mums share with their babies during pregnancy. Some mothers say that they 'know' the very moment they conceive; others, that they feel the baby 'fluttering' during the early weeks. Later, of course, you and your partner both will feel your baby's movements more and more intensely as she turns and presses against the wall of the uterus – though you only externally!

The first time a dad has direct physical contact with his baby is usually at birth, when your baby will be handed to you. Touching and holding such a tiny person can be daunting, and it is important for both you and your baby to be given ample opportunity to get in touch.

Fathers benefit from time spent with their babies, and massage can help you to develop your holding and handling skills. The following massage routine fosters trust between you and your baby and increases your confidence in your ability to change and bathe her and to help more with the daily responsibilities of childcare. Massage will also help to strengthen the physical and emotional relationship between you.

By learning how to handle your child better, you will be more able to soothe and comfort your baby at times when your partner needs to take a break. You can adapt the movements for any occasion when you are just sitting with your baby. Stroke her back and around her neck and shoulders as she sits on your lap.

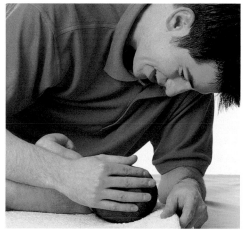

■ **TOP TIPS Give your partner a day off**
You can practice looking after your baby for longer and longer periods during the day, building up to the same amount of time that your partner would routinely spend with your baby while you are at work. Then give her the day off and, ideally, fit into her routine as if you had been called in to cover for her on a temporary basis. You'll see your child in a totally different light, observing her on a one-to-one basis over a period of time, watching her moods change and her daily pattern of living unfold – in short, a great bonding experience.

And you'll also come to appreciate, the hard way, the pressures of your partner's day. But whatever you do, don't see it as a competition. Your partner will really appreciate your attempt to better understand her life. So make sure you acknowledge how tough her job is and how you could never do it every day, unless, of course, you really do fancy yourself as a househusband.

1   Lay down on your side with your baby facing you, laying on her side. Using the relaxed weight of your whole right hand, start stroking your baby's upper back in a circular motion.

2   Then, take this movement down the length of your baby's spine smoothly, to include your baby's lower back.

3   Using the palm of your hand, gently stroke all around the crown of your baby's head in a slow, circular motion.

•   Repeat for as long as your baby is relaxed and comfortable.

household chores. So why not add an element of enjoyment to housework by taking your baby along with you? Put her in a baby carrier and chat away to her while you vacuum the carpets or do the washing up. This also allows your partner a break from babycare duties so that she can concentrate on other chores, spend time on herself or catch up on some sleep.

In any event, the daily care of your baby is a part of home life to which you can make an important contribution, improving relations with both your daughter and your partner. There's no reason why you can't undertake any of the babycare tasks that your partner usually does during the day, with the notable exception of breastfeeding. And the following chapters will guide you through all the basic jobs, step by step, with advice on how to make the most of the many bonding opportunities. Often these apparently mundane events in your baby's daily life can be surprisingly intimate occasions, so that even changing her nappy can become a very worthwhile experience!

Likewise, the routine of putting your baby to bed at night is a special time for you both, and one that dads should try to be involved in as much as possible. You can push this further, by aiming to gradually take on more and more of your baby's care in the evening, as she becomes increasingly independent and your partner is able to pull away. Eventually, you will be manning the frontline, responding to your baby's needs throughout the night, developing a strong father-son bond, and lifting a huge weight from your partner's shoulders, for which she will be forever grateful.

Carrying your baby around gives her the personal closeness and security she needs, and plenty of welcome stimulation to stop her feeling bored. Don't forget that carriers have uses inside the home as well; they are a great way to keep your baby close while doing chores.

WE NEED TO TALK | ABOUT HOUSEHOLD CHORES

A common area for disagreements is the responsibility for household chores. It might seem difficult to accept but, looking at it objectively, there cannot be a simple division between you going out to do paid work and your partner staying in and doing all the housework. Taking care of the baby is a full-time job in itself, which means that shopping, cooking, house cleaning, washing and ironing, for example, should be seen as tasks to share between you. If not, you are heading for a serious confrontation as your partner becomes increasingly worn out and resentful.

Pay what you can afford to buy in some help around the house. Even a cleaner for a couple of hours a week would mean that the kitchen and bathroom were properly cleaned, leaving you free to concentrate on daily essentials such as doing the dishes. It will be money well spent.

4

What can I do for my baby?

Holding and handling

One of the most frequent questions you will be asking in the first weeks is 'What can I do?' Maybe you should be asking 'What can I do for my baby?' Clearly, your partner needs as much help and support as possible, but your role is about more than keeping the house clean and cooking the odd meal. You need as much physical contact with your baby as possible, to build and maintain a bond.

But it can be difficult at first to get to grips with holding and handling your baby, especially when this appears to come so naturally to his mother. This chapter shows you the basic techniques of safe holding and handling, so you can be sure that you are doing them correctly. Now you can really enjoy holding your baby close and will become more confident every time you pick him up.

Picking up your baby

The first key point is to make sure that you are in the correct position for lifting your baby. Your baby may seem incredibly small and light right now, but if you get into the habit of lifting properly from the beginning, you will do so instinctively by the time he puts on enough weight to really make you feel it in the small of your back.

LIFTING YOUR BABY

1   Be sure to always support your baby's neck and bottom when moving him. Bring your face down close to your baby's and gently wake him if he's sleeping. Slide one hand under his neck, supporting his head, and one hand beneath his bottom. Talking quietly to your baby will help keep him calm as you lift.

2   Take your baby's weight in your hands and look into his eyes as you slowly raise him from the surface. Keep his head slightly above the level of the rest of his body.

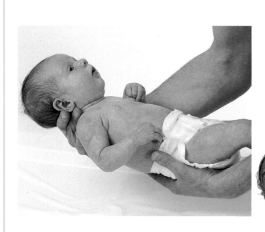

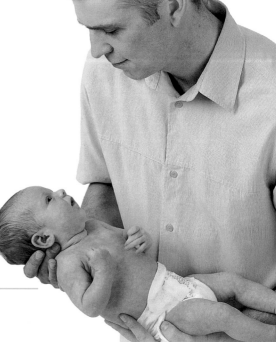

The worst thing you can do to your spine is to twist and bend it at the same time, so always try to position yourself in line with your baby, with his feet pointing towards you and your legs slightly apart. Keep your back as straight as possible but bend your knees so that your thighs take the strain rather than your spine. Keeping your baby close to you as you return to a standing position will reduce the strain on your back while reassuring him.

It is far easier to lift a baby who is lying face up – the recommended position in any event (see page 66) – than face down. But if your baby is lying prone, gently roll him over into a

3 Bringing him in close to your chest, move the hand supporting his bottom up his back to support his head as well. Then bend your other arm across so that his head rests in the crook of your arm, with your two wrists crossing over each other near the middle of his back, and his bottom rests on your forearm.

RULES OF BABY HANDLING

- Always support your baby's head and neck.
- Always support your baby's spine.
- Keep your baby's head in line with the rest of his body.
- Keep your baby close, talking to him and stroking him while you do so.
- Bend your knees when lifting your baby.

LAYING DOWN YOUR BABY

1 From a cradling position, gently slide your arms apart so that one hand supports your baby's head and neck, while the other supports his bottom. Slowly move him away from your body and over a padded surface.

2 Turn your baby's body so that it is in line with your own. Bend close to the changing mat or mattress and slowly lower him onto the surface, putting his bottom down first.

3 Once he has made contact with the surface, gently ease your supporting hand from underneath his bottom, then lower his upper body and head. Keep his head well supported until it is resting comfortably on the surface, before gently sliding your hand away.

position that is easier for you, before trying to pick him up.

Laying down your baby

Once you have picked up your baby, at some point you are going to have to lay him down. This is not a development that is likely to please your baby, who naturally wants to stay as warm and close to you as possible. So break the news gently, talking to him softly and stroking him reassuringly.

Laying a baby down can be just as hazardous as picking him up. The key thing to remember is to avoid placing him on anything other than a soft (but not smothering), secure surface, from which he cannot roll or slide off. As well as protecting him while lying down, this approach means that if he does slip from your grasp while being lowered, at least he will have a soft landing. As your baby grows stronger, you may find that you loosen your grip as he nears the surface and he will roll out of your arms, especially if he is upset at being laid down.

As with picking up, it's just as important to minimise the strain on your back when you lay your baby down. Remember to keep your feet apart, bend at the knees and hold him close to your chest as you lower him to a soft surface.

HOLDING A YOUNGER BABY

Resting against your shoulder is the most obvious and comfortable way to hold your baby. As with lifting, you need to support his bottom and neck, one with each hand. Your baby is nestled closely within your body shape, protected from bumps and bruises as you move around. This position is particularly comforting for the baby because he can hear your heartbeat.

Holding a baby face down in your arms can provide a welcome rest for tired arms and a change of view for your baby. It also may be good for colic. Support his head with the crook of your elbow while supporting the length of his body with your forearm. Your other arm slides through his legs until your hand is resting on his stomach.

Holding your baby

This is something that you are going to be spending a lot of time doing, especially during the first year of your baby's life, so it's important to get the basics right quickly. There are just a handful of recognised techniques for holding a child safely in your arms – depending on his age – so it's best to stick to these.

No doubt you will feel nervous at first, but holding your child will soon become second nature. On the other hand, that's the time when you may hit a few problems. It's easy to become complacent and start doing things while carrying your baby that you would never have done during your nervous first few weeks, especially if you're in a rush and juggling several tasks. For example, you might be picking up a steaming kettle or saucepan, stretching to reach something, or even talking on the telephone – all of which put you in a position where your mind is not totally on your baby.

In particular, it's important to be aware of the position of your baby's head in relation to your own body. When walking and carrying your baby in your arms, be careful to keep his head tucked into your body or at least keep your hand over the back of his head. It's very easy to forget that there is an extra piece of humanity sticking out as you move through hallways, doorways and close to other household objects at your baby's level, which can give him a nasty bash on the head. Also, while you may feel safe in the way that you are holding him, what if you tripped up or somebody else bumped in to you?

Your baby has no concept of the danger of falling and, as he grows stronger, he will struggle to force himself out of your grip. Sometimes, he will literally flip backwards and end up on the floor if you're not ready for it. So take care to keep a hand or arm across his back, especially when walking on stairs.

HOLDING AN OLDER BABY

Facing forwards Once your baby is able to support herself, this allows her more freedom to move and look around. Support your baby with her back against your chest, one arm under her arm and your hand across her chest. Your other hand supports her bottom.

On your hip She sits on the top of your hip, with her legs wrapped around on either side of your body. Use one arm to support her bottom while your free hand provides extra support around her back.

Cleaning and bathing

Helping to keep your baby clean is a great way to get involved in her care. Cleaning and bathing can be very intimate tasks that your baby will enjoy more and more as you work through the first months. It's also very fulfilling for you, and can be a duty that your partner may be reluctant to give up!

Bathing might seem daunting at first. Clearly, there is a lot of potential for things to go wrong when you add a large amount of water to a scenario that already involves undressing, nappy changing and dressing. But you will soon find that filling and using a baby bath is a surprisingly quick operation. In fact,

you don't even need to use a bath until your baby is able to sit up unaided.

Cleaning your newborn

Your new baby spends most of her day protected from the environment by layers of vests, bodysuits and blankets, so does not have a great deal of opportunity to get herself dirty. Aside from the nappy area, she just needs a quick once-over to clean the more exposed parts of her body, in other words her face, neck, hands and feet.

As usual, it's best to lay out everything you might need within easy reach of where you will

CLEANING ROUTINE

Eyes and ears Wet some cotton wool with cooled boiled water and wipe each eye, above and below, from the inner to the outer corner. Use a different piece of cotton wool for each wipe and each eye, to reduce the chances of spreading infection. Use more cotton wool to clean around and behind the ears. Do not clean inside the ear, which is protected by a self-cleaning mucous membrane.

Neck This is a difficult area to clean unless you can distract your baby into looking elsewhere, so that

she inadvertently exposes the front of her neck. Wipe clean with wet cotton wool and pat dry with a soft cloth to reduce the chances of blackneck occurring.

Hands Unclench your baby's hands to check for dirt between the fingers and underneath the nails. Wipe and pat dry as before.

Feet Now clean the top and bottom of your baby's feet, and between her toes, gently easing them apart, where necessary. Pat dry with a towel.

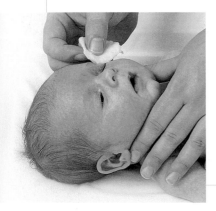
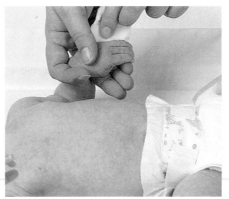

be cleaning your baby – ideally a warm place with plenty of room for manoeuvre. You need a bowl of cooled boiled water, cotton wool, and a soft towel or cloth, plus a bowl to hold the used cotton wool.

A safe and convenient way of doing this is to put your baby's changing mat on the floor, spread a towel over it and lay your baby on top. An added advantage is that your baby virtually dries herself as you go along, and you simply wrap the towel around her when the cleaning is complete.

The key to giving your baby a proper clean is to get inside the numerous folds of skin where dirt and perspiration are easily trapped, causing soreness. One such area is the neck, particularly under the chin, or chins, which commonly suffers a condition called blackneck – literally the growth of what looks like mould within the skin folds.

How to bath your baby

The easiest way to bath your baby is in a plastic baby bath specially made for the purpose. Choose a warm room, perhaps even the bathroom, and place the bath on the floor, ideally on a waterproof surface, such as a plastic sheet. Place her fresh clothes and nappy within

Stomach and legs A wriggling baby can make this area difficult to access. Wipe her tummy with more wet cotton wool, then use new wool to start on the folds where her legs meet her torso. Wipe down along the creases and away from her body to avoid transmitting infections to the genital area (this is particularly important for a girl). Pat dry with a soft cloth or towel, checking that no moisture is trapped in the folds.

Cleaning a girl Lift her bottom slighting by raising both her ankles gently with one hand. Using fresh cotton wool, clean the outer lips of her vulva – but don't clean inside. Always wipe downward. Then, keeping her bottom raised, clean her buttocks using fresh cotton wool. Clean the backs of her thighs and up her back, if necessary. Dry the whole area thoroughly.

Cleaning a boy Using fresh cotton wool, wipe his penis using a downward motion – don't pull the foreskin back. Clean around his testicles as well. Holding your baby's ankles, lift his bottom gently and clean his anal area and the backs of his thighs. Pat the whole area thoroughly dry.

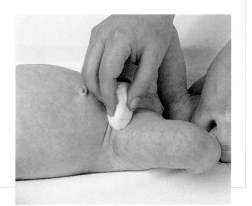

BATHING ROUTINE

Lower your baby into the water Kneel close to the bath, cradling your baby in your arms. Support her bottom with one hand and her head and shoulders with the other. Lower her in to the water, putting her bottom down first.

Wash her chest and stomach Always support your baby's head and shoulders while in the bath, gripping her gently under the arm to prevent her from slipping down into the water or rolling over. With your arm behind her, wash her chest and stomach.

Wash her neck and back Next, sit her up, supporting her from the front. Wash the back of her neck and the upper back area.

Rinse her lower back Tip her further forward, taking care to keep her face out of the water, and rinse her lower back and bottom.

Lift her out Lean her back into the starting position and, using the same grip as you used to lower her in, lift her out, supporting her head, shoulders and bottom.

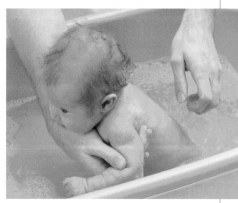

Dry her Place her on a towel spread over a changing mat and wrap her up to keep warm, but avoid covering her face. Pat her dry.

WASHING YOUR BABY'S HAIR

Although many babies will only need their hair rinsed while in the bath, you may feel that your baby's locks really need a proper wash. The simplest way of doing this is to lay her along one arm, wrapped in a towel, with her head over a baby bath filled with warm water. Rinse her hair with your free hand. Pat dry with a towel.

easy reach, but not so close that they can be splashed with bath water.

If you have to use an adult tub, there are products available in which to safely lay or sit your baby – even an inflatable, floating bed – but baby baths let you attend to your baby comfortably from a kneeling position rather than you having to stretch over the high sides of a tub, which is also a more hazardous and unforgiving environment for the baby.

Don't get carried away with the amount of water you put in the tub – never more than 5-7 cm, or over waist height when she is able to sit up. Babies can drown in a tiny amount of water so *never* leave your baby unattended.

Use a temperature gauge to check that the water is about body temperature – 37° C (98.6°F). As you become more experienced, you can use your elbow to test the water, but it will always be safer to use a gauge. Keep checking the bath water because it can quickly turn cold.

Avoid scented soaps and bubble baths. There really is no need to use anything but water, otherwise you are simply increasing the risk of irritating your baby's very sensitive skin. Add cold water to the bath first, then warm, to eliminate any chance of a scalding injury.

If you want to rinse your baby's hair, it's probably best to do so just before you put her in the bath. Hold her along one arm with her head over the bath and pour water over her hair with your other, cupped hand. Try to prevent water running on to her face and eyes. Under a year old, your baby doesn't need any shampoo. When she's older, add a small amount of specially mild baby shampoo to the bath water and gently rub it in.

Once in the bath, there is a simple washing routine to follow (see left). Try talking and singing to your baby all the time to help keep her calm. Afterwards, lift her straight out of the bath onto a towel placed over the changing mat, which provides a soft, safe and waterproof surface for drying.

Looking after your baby's teeth

Babies usually start producing teeth at around six months of age but some can begin as early as three months or as late as 12 months.

Your baby will eventually develop 20 teeth by the age of two and a half. These milky white teeth are very important, not just because they enable her to eat, but the way they help her to speak, and pave the way for her second, permanent set of teeth. The first set will start to fall out around the age of six years, to be replaced by 32 stronger teeth that will last, hopefully, for the rest of her life.

Keeping her teeth clean is obviously an important operation and it's best to get into the habit early – a good job for dads. It's also vital to limit the amount of sugary foods your baby eats, especially drinks on which she may suck for a long time. Acidic fruit juices can lead to craters in the surface of your baby's teeth, and apple juice is a particular culprit. So always dilute these drinks to be more like flavoured water. Raw fruit and vegetables are great for children's teeth because they are naturally sweet and gnawing on them can help clean and strengthen teeth.

TOOTH CARE

Cleaning one or two teeth with a cloth Gently wipe your baby's first teeth and gums with a piece of gauze to remove the plaque, acid and bacteria that cause tooth decay. You also can use cotton buds.

Brushing teeth day and night Sit your baby on your lap and carefully brush her teeth and gums. A gentle up and down motion will remove any build-up of plaque. Be particularly careful while brushing her back teeth in case you make her gag or hit a sensitive part of the throat with the brush.

Nappy changing

If you really want to play an active part in the care of your child, then changing nappies is a great opportunity to literally get your hands dirty. One of the best things about it is that it gives you valuable one-on-one time with your child. Done in the right way, this much-maligned and essential job can prove to be a real bonding experience.

Cloth or disposable?

By far, the most popular choice of nappy is the disposable kind, which are very absorbent, quick and easy to use, come in a wide range of styles and sizes, and, of course, can simply be dropped into the bin after each change.

The alternative is to try re-usable cloth nappies, which now come in a wide range of styles, with poppers or Velcro® fastenings. This route has higher start-up costs but should provide savings over the long term as you continue to re-use the nappies – especially if you are planning more children.

In practical terms, cloth nappies will usually have to be changed more regularly because they are not as absorbent as disposables, but regular changing means your baby is less likely to suffer nappy rash. On average, over the first 2½ years of life, a baby will go through 4-6 disposables or 6-12 cloth nappies a day. You can buy paper liners to minimise the soiling of a cloth nappy but there's no denying that it's a messy business, and keeping used nappies in a solution-filled bucket until they can be washed is a perilous affair. One way of avoiding much of this unpleasantness is to use a weekly laundry service, which collects your dirty nappies and leaves a fresh supply in its place. You could use cloth nappies during the day or when at home, and disposables at night or when out.

Changing places

For a young baby, taking him off to a quiet, warm place, such as a nursery or bathroom, is the best way to keep him relaxed and ensure some quality time for you both. The safest place for the operation is on a sponge-filled changing mat, left on the floor to avoid any danger of the baby rolling off a high surface, but a young baby (one who has not learned to roll over), can be changed on an waist-high surface. Then the golden rule is to have plenty of everything you need – cotton balls and lukewarm water or unfragranced wipes and, if you are using disposables, special scented bags for dirty ones – close at hand and ready to use. Events move very quickly once the nappy comes off!

Jack's story

The last thing I expected was for nappy changing to be something that I enjoyed. But it was a rare chance for me to be alone with my son – an intimate time. He was usually full of smiles, gurgling away, and enjoying the extra attention. I also felt that I was actively contributing to his care; the worse the state of his nappies, the greater the satisfaction when the job was done. I felt good about it, especially when we were with other people and I took him off for a change. One of my proudest moments was changing him late at night without waking him up, when my partner and I desperately needed sleep.

NAPPY CHANGING ROUTINE*

Make sure you have everything you need, open and ready to use, in a quiet place. Don't forget to keep a few small toys close by to help distract your baby for the final few seconds of the job. All the time you are changing the nappy, talk and sing to your baby, maintaining eye contact as much as possible, rubbing and tickling his arms, legs and feet in a gentle massage.

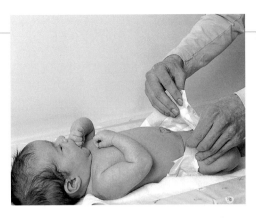

1   Lay your baby face up on the mat, taking care to support his head and the base of his spine as you lower him down. If he's dressed, strip him down to his undershirt or just his nappy.

2   Unfasten the tabs and slide the nappy away, using an unsoiled area to give a first wipe. Baby boys are likely to urinate shortly after a nappy is removed, in reaction to the cooler air. Drop a tissue or wipe onto the penis to deflect the flow, or, if the nappy is only wet, hold it over the genital area until the danger time has passed.

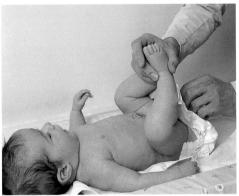

3   Roll up the nappy with one hand (keep the other on your baby) and place it where your baby can't kick it. Now clean carefully (see page 35) within all the skin folds and use different wipes for the genital areas and bottom to avoid spreading infection. Pat dry, particularly in the folds where soreness can develop.

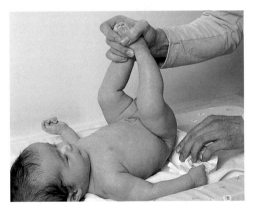

4   Spread out a fresh nappy; slide it underneath your baby, and secure at the sides. Once your baby is dressed, place the disposable into a bag and throw it away or place a soiled cloth nappy into a holding bucket.

*   This method works for both disposables and for shaped, Velcro®- or popper-closing cloth nappies.

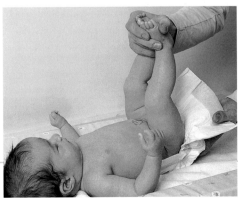

Dressing your baby

Dressing your baby can be a real pleasure but it also can be tricky fitting a wriggly baby into an outfit, and there always seems to be one more popper than you need. How does that happen?

Your baby will spend most of her infant life in the short-sleeved, legless bodysuit, better known as a vest, and the all-in-one bodysuit, known as a babygro. Choose ones made of soft, natural fibres, that are hardwearing but comfortable, and with room for growth.

Vests

The best type of vest joins at the crotch with poppers, preventing it from riding up your

baby's back and letting in cold draughts. Envelope necklines are also a must-have. They pull over your baby's head and also slip down

PUTTING ON AND TAKING OFF A VEST ROUTINE

Ease the vest over her head Lay your baby on a warm, padded surface and gather the material together at the neck of the vest with both hands. Slip the vest behind her head, stretching the opening wide. Gently raise her head. Position the opening over the crown of her head and gently pull the vest over her head and neck.

Place her arms in the sleeves Straighten the fabric around her neck. Take one sleeve, gather up the material in one hand and hold with your thumb inside the arm. With your other hand, gently take

hold of your baby's wrist and ease the sleeve over her hand and down her arm. Repeat with the other sleeve.

Do up the poppers Gently smooth the fabric down over her front. Lift her bottom slightly to slide the tail of the suit underneath and up through her legs. Start with the outermost poppers on the same side, front and back. You can then work along the poppers, confident that there will not be one left over.

To remove a clean vest (upwards) Lay your baby on a warm, padded surface and undo the poppers. Slide

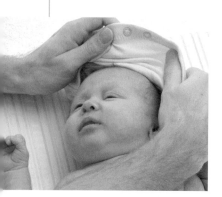

over her shoulders to be pulled off over her legs. This can be a lifesaver when the bottom of her vest is soiled and you don't want to pull it over her head.

Babies have difficulty controlling their body temperature, so it's important to bear the environment in mind when deciding what clothes to put on. A basic guideline is to always give your baby one more layer than you are wearing. Layers of thin clothes are better than one thick item, simply because you can more easily control a baby's temperature by reducing or increasing the layers as necessary. A hat is also essential in autumn and winter because babies lose a large amount of heat through their heads. In summer, your baby also will need a hat to shade her from the sun.

Always dress your baby somewhere warm and comfortable, and make sure you have everything you need to hand. You can use this one-to-one time to strengthen your bond, talking, nuzzling and gently massaging her. Try to maintain eye contact as much as possible and use the clothes as props to entertain, for example, with a game of peek-a-boo. Make the experience as enjoyable as possible for both of you, without making it overlong to the point where your baby becomes cold or bored.

the vest up her body. Gather up a sleeve in one hand and use your other hand to gently guide her arm out of the sleeve. Repeat with the other sleeve. Gather up the vest at your baby's neck, stretching the opening as wide as possible to avoid dragging the material over her face. Pull the vest up over her face to the crown of her head in one smooth motion. Gently lift her head to remove the vest.

To remove a dirty vest (downwards) Remove the soiled nappy and give your baby's bottom a quick clean. Gently lift up her head. Stretch a corner of the neckline over one shoulder and repeat on the other side. Lay her back down and slide the neck opening down each arm. Stretch open the neckline again and gently lift her arms from each sleeve. Gather up the vest material and slide it down her legs, aiming to avoid any further soiling. You can now finish cleaning your baby and replace her nappy and clothes.

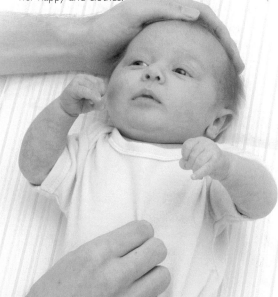

Bodysuits

The all-in-one bodysuit is a great piece of kit for babies. Bodysuits keep babies warm and comfortable all over, and make life easy for parents because you only need to find one item of clothing when changing your baby's nappy or getting her ready for bed. These suits can be worn 24 hours a day when your baby is very young, and make excellent pyjamas for when she is older.

Some bodysuits come with a zip on the front that makes them very quick and easy to put on, but the risk of catching skin or body parts mean that it's best to stick to poppers. However, after many washes, the suits tend to stretch and it becomes virtually impossible to match them all up.

When choosing bodysuits, be aware that age sizes vary widely from one maker to another and the only reasonable guide is your baby's height and weight. Always try to allow for stretching and growing room.

Few babies enjoy the chore of undressing, partly because of the temperature change and also because they just don't like change. So follow the usual rules of giving reassurance and making it as enjoyable an experience as possible for you both.

WE NEED TO TALK | ABOUT SHARING CHORES

In the early months of your baby's life it can seem that she constantly needs her nappy changed and a new set of clothes to wear. It's a lot of work, which can become very irritating, especially when it happens just as you're starting to relax again after the last change. Inevitably, these tasks are going to cause friction in the household, and you will feel the chill of many icy stares from your partner if she feels that you are a little too slow to put down your newspaper and help. A good way around this is to divide the responsibility for changes between the two of you over the course of the week. For example, she does the morning shift while you get ready for work, but you take over as soon as you return in the evening. Alternatively, your partner could do all week while you do the weekend. Obviously, these are artificial boundaries and regularly there will be good reasons to break them, but at least if you discuss the issue, and your partner feels that you are making a commitment, then there is less likely to be ongoing friction.

PUTTING ON AND TAKING OFF
A BODYSUIT ROUTINE

Prepare the suit Open all of the poppers and spread the bodysuit out on a soft, warm surface. Lay your baby on top of the suit.

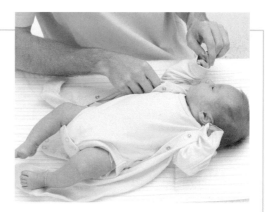

Put in her arms Gather up the sleeve material and gently slide it over your baby's wrists, taking care to ensure that her fingers or nails are not caught up in the process. You may need to stretch the tight wrists of the suit to fit her hands through.

Put in her legs Taking each leg in turn, gather up the material and slide in her foot until her toes reach the end. Then run the material fully up her legs.

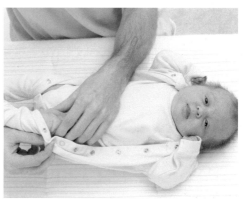

Fasten the poppers Line up the two sides of the bodysuit on your baby's front and fasten the poppers from the top down to the crotch. This is the easiest part of the suit to fasten and stops your baby wriggling out while you attend to the legs. Fasten the leg poppers from the ankle up to the crotch, and then do the other leg, again starting from the ankle.

To remove the suit
The easiest way to remove a suit is from the toes upwards; your baby will probably kick out her legs as soon as those poppers are undone. Undo all the poppers on the suit and support each knee as you ease off the material. Lift up your baby's bottom and slide the lower half of the suit up her back. Support your baby's elbow and, without tugging, remove each arm from its sleeve. If the bottom half is soiled, you may want to start at the arms and work downwards.

Feeding

Breastfeeding

There is no doubt about it: breastfeeding is the best possible start in life for your baby. There is a long list of potential benefits for your child's health and development, and medical research is constantly finding new reasons to feed naturally. Breastfeeding also benefits your partner's long-term health, helps her return more quickly to her pre-pregnancy shape, and nurtures the close bond between mother and baby.

Breastfeeding is also far less work – there are no bottles to clean, no formula milk to prepare, and at night it's much easier for you – and your partner – if she can just roll over and breastfeed the baby back to sleep.

Having said that, there are certain situations where breastfeeding may be difficult, for example, if there is a pre-existing physical condition, or is inadvisable (if she is on certain medication), or, just as importantly, a woman feels strongly that she doesn't want to breastfeed. And even where a woman is committed to breastfeeding, she may find it hard to master the right technique, or illness or other situations may interfere.

So making the decision between breast and bottlefeeding is by no means straightforward, and even if a woman chooses to do so, it does not always turn out how she expected. Many women who start breastfeeding give up within six weeks of the birth. In the UK, only about 25 per cent of mothers still breastfeed at six months – a much lower rate than anywhere in Europe. In Norway, for example, 80 per cent of mothers are still breastfeeding after six months.

If your partner dearly wants to breastfeed but finds herself unable to do so, this can be a big psychological blow and she will need all your understanding and support. Premature, special-care and even adopted babies have been successfully breastfed, so make sure that you and your partner check out all the help available.

Breastfeeding can sometimes make fathers feel shut out from the close bonding that takes place during feeds. But when your partner feels ready, she can express milk, which you then can feed to your baby in a bottle, or you can give him an occasional bottle of formula milk or water (if your health visitor recommends it). Until then, let mum and baby get on with the breastfeeding while you enjoy the peace and quiet. Of course, you can always help by fetching your baby when he's ready to be fed and putting him back to bed when he's finished.

Despite all the benefits of breastfeeding, bringing up your baby on formula milk is not a disaster – far from it. Formula milk provides all the nourishment your child needs and can actually contain more nutrients than breast milk. But babies can absorb nutrients more quickly from breastmilk, so that's not really an issue. The big difference is that a mother's milk contains a variety of extra ingredients, which kill bacteria, fight infections, and generally strengthen a baby's immune system.

But whatever the facts and figures, and however strongly you may feel about a particular method of feeding, the final decision will be down to your partner – it's her body. Of course, you should be involved in the discussion, but once it's made, she needs your full support and should not be made to feel guilty about her chosen route.

Either way, feeding time is a pleasure not to be missed. And even when your baby is being breastfed, you can feel a real sense of involvement simply by watching and encouraging. It's a fascinating process to witness, and many

BREASTFEEDING IN PUBLIC

Surveys have shown that up to 60 per cent of women have been made to feel uncomfortable while trying to publically breastfeed their babies. Even bottlefeeding mums have been asked to stop. In the UK this has become such a problem that Scotland has introduced a law to prevent discrimination; England is expected to follow suit. Concern about feeding in public places is a key reason for mothers stopping breastfeeding early so they really need your support.

babies develop bizarre habits in their movements and noises as they feed, which can make it very entertaining and bring the whole family together in a mutual bonding session.

Bottlefeeding your baby

Choosing to bottlefeed your baby means that you and your partner will need to commit to high levels of cleanliness in all aspects of the feeding process. Of course, everything you do for your baby in the early stages of life should

WE NEED TO TALK | ABOUT HOW TO FEED THE BABY

If you are keen to have a say on whether your baby will be breast- or bottlefed, research shows that the decision is often made early in the pregnancy or even before conception. A big influence on the woman's decision is her perception of what her partner feels about breastfeeding, and a desire to involve him in the care of the baby. So it's important for you to make sure your partner understands your feelings as early as possible, and that you are both fully aware of the advantages and disadvantages of each method.

be aimed at maintaining his health and avoiding illness, but feeding him requires extra vigilance to prevent some of the more nasty infections.

As a father, you may not be as involved in the feeding and bonding activities as you would like, but helping to prepare the necessary equipment each day can be a huge benefit to your partner and also give you extra satisfaction from making a contribution.

Once all the feeding equipment has been thoroughly washed, you will need to sterilise everything. There are various ways of doing this and it's no longer believed essential to boil the bottles. There are special sterilising kits using chemicals to do the job, or you can invest in a steam cleaner. Alternatively there are bottles that can be sterilised in a microwave oven, or you could use a dishwasher on a hot cycle, which has the added benefit of allowing you to clean as many bottles as you need for the day.

Making up formula milk

Once you have sterilised all the bottlefeeding equipment and washed your hands, you can start mixing the formula. It's usually based on cow's milk or soya, and can be bought readymade in cartons, though it's far more common, and more economical, to buy powder and mix the milk as you need it.

As well as keeping everything scrupulously clean, you also need to follow the manufacturer's instructions very carefully. In particular, how you measure the amounts of water and powder is crucial: if there's not enough water your baby can become dehydrated, but if there's too much he could be under-nourished. So as a precaution, never heap up or pack down a scoop of formula, and match every scoop with the correct amount of water.

It's a good idea to make up several bottles at once and store them in the fridge until you need them, but bear in mind that you have to throw away any unused milk within 24 hours. When you take the milk out to use, either let it warm naturally to room temperature or stand it in a jug of hot water.

How to feed your baby

It's feeding time again, only this time it's you who will be delivering the milk to your eager offspring. If your partner is breastfeeding and has expressed milk for you to bottlefeed the baby, then you have probably been taking a keen interest in the feeding ritual for three or four weeks. This is a good period of time to

---

THE BENEFITS OF BREASTFEEDING

The World Health Organisation recommends that babies are exclusively breastfed for the first six months of life.

Babies who are breastfed suffer fewer chest, ear, gastric and urinary infections; have healthier hearts, improved brain development; a lower risk of environmental allergies; protection against diabetes, and improved bone development.

They have also been found to develop higher levels of intelligence and be more upwardly socially mobile in later life.

Breastfeeding mothers have a reduced risk of ovarian and breast cancer, experience greater weight loss if they breastfeed for at least six months and a quicker return to their pre-pregnancy shapes, and a reduced risk of osteoporosis in later life.

Fathers benefit, too. Partners and babies are healthier, it's much less work than bottlefeeding, and it's free.

There's even good for taxpayers. It's reckoned that in the USA, $3.6 billion a year would be saved on the cost of treating three common childhood infections if 50 per cent of mothers breastfed for 6 months (this is double the current rate).

STERILISING BOTTLES ROUTINE

Wash the bottles You will need a bottle brush to ensure a really thorough wash. Fill a clean bowl with hot soapy water and immerse the bottles. Pay special attention to the screw thread at the top of the bottle and the inside of the neck, these are the areas where hardened milk can easily become lodged. Rinse thoroughly to prevent any build up of left-over detergent.

Wash the teats Use a special teat brush to get right in to all the tricky corners. Turn the teat inside out to finish the job and then rinse thoroughly.

Follow the manufacturer's instructions When using sterilising equipment, always follow instructions to minimise the chances of any bacteria slipping through. Once the sterilisation is complete, drain the container. You may have to rinse the items with cooled boiled water if using sterilizer tablets. You can use the bottles to feed your baby immediately or leave them in the steriliser.

MAKING UP FORMULA ROUTINE

Boil the water Fill a kettle with fresh or filtered water and boil. Do not use mineral water or softened water, because the level of mineral salts can be unsuitable for babies. Pour the correct amount of cooled, boiled water into the bottle.

Measure the formula Use the scoop provided to measure out the required amount of formula, then level off any excess powder with leveler or a knife – scraping across the scoop, not patting down.

Mix and store Double check the amount of scoops you need and add them to the bottle. Add seal and screw on the cap. Now shake the bottle hard so that the water and powder are thoroughly mixed. Replace seal with sterilized teat. You can make up several bottles at once; store them in the fridge for up to 24 hours.

allow your partner to properly establish the breastfeeding process. Even if she has been bottlefeeding from birth, it's probably best to wait until she feels she has developed a strong enough bond with the baby before you start feeding him as well.

Feeding your baby should be an intimate experience, guaranteed to help the pair of you bond. Watch your partner to see how she relates to your baby while feeding and try to recreate that special atmosphere. Sit down, make yourself comfortable – you'll be there for some time – and perhaps put on some easy-going music to help you relax and enjoy the experience. Look into your baby's eyes and try to maintain eye contact throughout the feed to really connect with him, smiling and encouraging him as you go along.

Winding your baby

Babies will usually swallow some air while feeding, especially when taking milk from a bottle because it is not always easy for them to make a tight seal around the teat with their mouths. Air can form bubbles in your baby's stomach, causing discomfort and a feeling of fullness, so you need to help your baby expel the air by winding, or burping.

Some babies need winding more than others, and you may also find that a differently shaped teat can ease the problem. But if your baby simply falls asleep after a feed, there's no need to disturb him. In fact, your baby will often drift off to sleep after feeding, just as you might after a big lunch. His eyes will start rolling and he'll give the appearance of being intoxicated but it's a perfectly normal reaction.

As well as expelling air, your baby may also bring up milk that he has swallowed. Unlike vomiting, this spitting up is usually a dribble of milk from the mouth, which the baby hardly seems to notice. Sometimes it happens because of overfeeding, but generally it's a result of the valve at the top of the stomach not yet being

BOTTLE FEEDING ROUTINE

Warm the milk Use a pan of hot water or an electric bottle warmer to warm the milk (see box). Do not use a microwave. This heats the milk unevenly, leaving some parts too hot. Also, heating breastmilk in a microwave will destroy some of the ingredients that boost the baby's immune system.

Check the temperature Before giving the milk to your baby, shake a few drops on to the inside of your wrist. It should feel warm but not too hot.

Stroke his cheek (1) Let your baby see the bottle then stroke his cheek to prompt the rooting reflex. He will automatically turn to you with his mouth open ready to suck.

Offer the bottle (2) Hold the bottle at an angle of about 45 degrees so that its neck is full of milk and there are no air bubbles. Offer the teat to your baby and allow him to take it deep into his mouth and begin sucking.

Maintain the milk level (3) Keep the bottle steady so that he can properly latch on. You will feel him sucking on the bottle. Adjust the angle so that the top of the bottle is always full of milk.

Remove the bottle (4) When your baby has finished feeding, or you need to wind him, slip your little finger in to the corner of his mouth to break the suction. Once you have finished, throw away any unused milk and start the next feed with a fresh bottle.

WARMING MILK

Most parents prefer to warm bottled milk to make it more closely resemble breast milk. Most babies, however, don't mind it being cooler as long as the milk is at room temperature, not cold. Do not give a baby milk that has been left to warm for over an hour.

THREE WAYS TO WIND A BABY

On your shoulder Lift him up so that his head is over your shoulder and facing away from your neck. Use one hand to support his bottom and the other to gently rub or pat his back. You can also try starting at the base of his spine and moving upwards, to literally 'bring up' the trapped air.

Sitting up Raise your baby into a sitting position on your lap. Support his head with one hand while you use the other hand to gently rub or pat around his shoulder blades.

Across your knees Lay your baby down so that his stomach rests on one knee and his chest on the other, or on your crooked arm. His head should be facing away from you with nothing obstructing his mouth. Gently rub or pat his back.

strong enough to prevent fluids from rising back up. You can help ease the problem by holding your baby's body straight at a 30 degree angle during and after feeding, making it less likely that fluids will 'run out' from the top of his stomach.

There's no escaping the fact that feeding your baby can be a messy business well before she gets to the stage of throwing and spilling proper food and drink. So it's a good idea to lay a towel over your lap to protect your clothes, and put a bib on your baby to avoid having to change his outfit afterwards.

Feeding solids to your baby

By the time your baby is six to nine months old, he will be starting to develop new ways of communicating and you will begin to feel that a fuller relationship is now possible. It's also around this time that your baby will be ready to move on to solid foods, giving you a new opportunity to increase your involvement in your baby's care. Hopefully you will already have been preparing formula milk or giving him an occasional bottle of breast milk; now you can take it a step further.

And it's not only the feeding that you can help with. Just as you helped prepare bottles to ease the pressure on your partner and make a contribution, you could now actually cook some food for your baby.

Even if you're a terrible chef, it doesn't matter. Most recipes for babies are a very simple mix of nutritious ingredients, and the great thing is that you don't really need to worry about how the food looks when it reaches the table – by this stage everything has been well and truly mashed.

There are some great recipe books around with quick, healthy and fun food for children of all ages, so you should be able to find something that you can make and he will like to eat - just don't feel disheartened if your perfect pasta goes on the floor.

You will really help your partner in the kitchen, and save both of you time at mealtimes, by preparing a large batch of purée, putting it in to an ice cube tray and freezing it. Then take out as many cubes as you need for each meal and defrost accordingly. You also can freeze cubes of individual vegetables such as mashed potato, for example, and then make up meals from the pre-prepared selection. Be careful if you are defrosting in a microwave oven because the food will often heat unevenly, so don't forget to check and stir thoroughly to mix in any hotspots. Perhaps the best way is to simply put the food dish in a larger bowl of hot water and let it heat up gently to the required temperature.

Make feeding fun

Your baby will still have a very short attention span, so keeping him interested for long enough to eat a meal is never going to be easy. To make the most of every mealtime in terms of building your relationship, you really need to make it a fun experience.

Just as you do when changing nappies or bathing your baby, you need to maintain eye contact, keep smiling, talk and encourage him all the way. Let him see you taste the food and how much you enjoy it. Turn the feeding

process into play by making funny noises as you pop in the food. Try holding the spoon above your head and flying it down in to his mouth like an aeroplane, or pretend to be a train droving into his 'tunnel' mouth – both with accompanying special effects.

It's not a disaster if your baby doesn't eat the food – although it will be very frustrating for you – because he will always let you know when he is hungry. But if all else fails, point his high chair in the direction of his favourite TV programme. This can distract him to the point where he will hardly notice he is eating, as you help him get through the bowl on automatic pilot. Distracting him with a toy also can help.

One thing you can guarantee at mealtimes is a lot of mess: on your child, the floor, the furniture and you, so choose an appropriate place and never attempt feeding while in your work clothes. Give your baby a bib, or even a plastic vest, and place some newspaper or a plastic sheet on the floor. If you are planning to give him a bath that day, it's best to wait until after the meal! You may need one, too.

Spoonfeeding

It can take several weeks for your baby to master the technique of eating from a spoon. As with bottlefeeding, you will need to sterilise the spoon and bowl. Hold your baby in an upright position on your lap or in a suitable chair. Make sure he is wearing a bib and your lap is covered as well! Scoop up some purée in a long-handled spoon and hold it just between his lips so that he can suck the food off. Be careful not to put the food too far into his mouth in case he gags. Some of the food will probably reappear until he grows used to taking it off the spoon.

Helping your baby feed himself

The first rule of teaching your baby to feed himself is not to expect too much too soon. Many babies will not be able to master the movement of a spoon into a bowl and then into their mouths until they are beyond their first birthdays. Their physical and neurological development is often not up to the task of co-ordinating such a tricky operation, even though they may well be able to grab a spoon, scoop up some food and flick it across the room – which is much easier and much more fun.

Until he can properly use a spoon, the only other option is to use his hands (not that it gets much cleaner when he can use a spoon). Finger

feeding is messy and ineffective but it's important to let your baby feed himself if he wants to – and at his own pace. You can help once he becomes bored, but in the meantime, he needs to experiment to learn and it's a great way of developing his hand-eye co-ordination. Try giving him a spoon to play with in his free hand, while he eats individual baked beans, one by one, with the other.

Finger foods are obviously a great idea at this stage. Cubes of cooked vegetables, strips of peeled fruit, seedless grapes, pieces of cooked pasta, chunks of cheese and, of course, sandwiches. But avoid nuts and food with seeds.

A plastic spoon can be a dangerous tool in the hands of a small baby so it's best to choose one with softened edges, which will not hurt too much when jabbed into little gums and tonsils. You also can buy heat sensitive baby spoons that change colour when the food is too hot to eat.

Don't be worried if your baby doesn't take to your food immediately. Often, a baby will appear totally disinterested at first, only to clean the bowl as soon as you turn your back. If you are feeding your baby in a high chair, it's worth

getting him used to sitting in it before you introduce him to solid foods, otherwise you are contending with two new experiences at same time. Once he is feeding regularly in the chair, you will probably need to keep him out of it until the food is ready. This will help to prevent him from becoming bored and screaming to get out just as the food arrives.

Choosing a high chair is an important decision, given the impact that good or bad mealtimes can have on your day. The first priorities are to find a chair that is secure and stable, holds your baby comfortably in place, and is easy to clean. Double-check the quality of the harness straps, particularly the locking mechanism, and be aware that these quickly become covered in food so it's best to find removable ones that can be thrown into the washing machine.

Ideally, your chair will have a detachable tray, which again makes it easy to clean and also allows greater flexibility in how you use the chair. Eating meals together is an excellent way of developing a family bond, helps make your baby more sociable from an early age, and encourages discipline in the long term –

something you will really appreciate once you start taking him to restaurants. So check how the high chair would work with the family table that you are most likely to use for meals with the baby. Your baby should be able to sit in the high chair and feed directly from the table like the rest of the family.

As your child comes to rely less on milk for his nourishment, he will need to drink more liquid to avoid becoming dehydrated. Try to limit his drinks to water or diluted, unsweetened fruit juice. Apple juice is particularly acidic and will quickly erode the surface of your child's teeth if not watered down to, say, one part juice to 10 parts water. When switching from bottles, you may find that your baby will not drink from his new training cup. It's simply a question of trial and error until you find the style of cup, with the right flow of liquid, to satisfy your baby.

Richard's story

When our son first started to feed himself, I'd be shocked to come in from work and find the boy literally drenched in sauce, with food all over the floor, the table, and my wife. I kept complaining that she was exacerbating the situation with all the sloppy food she was giving him but she said he needed to try out different things.

The day he had his first bowl of spaghetti, he ate it with his hands, dangling the strings from above his head and trying to catch the ends in his mouth. His whole face was covered in tomato sauce and I hardly recognised him through the wig of pasta stuck to his forehead. But my son, who was by now concentrating very hard on some strawberries, was clearly loving every minute. It was hilarious. When I thought about it later I realised that I just had to loosen up. My wife was right – he needed to explore food. Once I relaxed, feeding him at weekends became something to look forward to, just as it should be with any good meal.

Amusing your baby

Every month will see big changes in your baby's range of skills and what she finds interesting. Her eyesight is limited at first but brightly coloured objects will help occupy her in the cot, and a mobile is always a good idea. Newborns particularly respond to red and black objects, so try to find appropriate toys that combine these colours.

Life is a constant learning experience for your baby and every time she makes a new noise or movement, sees something from a different angle or with a different use, or hears new sounds and voices, it will be a source of fascination for her. The more you can stimulate her interest and allow her to see and feel different things, the quicker she will develop her skills. But at the same time, too much fun and activity may simply overload her.

There is little need to spend money on expensive toys when your baby is young because she only has a tiny attention span and will quickly lose interest. Common household objects can be just as much fun. Likewise, the simplest tricks that you can perform for her, such as rolling a ball, can leave her transfixed. If you or others do want to buy special items, interactive toys are the most long-lasting, with lots of noises and moving parts to keep babies interested and help them develop new skills. But always check for removable parts that could be a choking hazard, and avoid anything so small that it could be swallowed or become lodged in her throat – once a baby is able to pick up things and put them in her mouth, she will practice doing so constantly!

SIMPLE GAMES

There are lots of simple games that you can play with your baby, which will be great fun for you both while at the same time helping to develop her language, vision, memory and co-ordination skills. Babies love repetition, so pulling faces, singing songs and rhymes, and peeping over your hands, can all keep her entertained. Combine these with a tickle at the end of each action or verse and she will hardly be able to contain herself as she waits for the inevitable finale. Encourage her to mimic your actions and sounds – the ability to do so is a strong sign of her developing intelligence. Animal noises are great for this because she can link the noise with your impersonation and pictures in a book. And don't forget to read to her. From the earliest age your baby will enjoy hearing the rhythms of your voice and looking at the pictures, because every page holds a new experience for her.

Crawl for it By about six months most babies enjoy lying prone. They can push up onto their arms and shift their weight to stretch out and grasp toys. Try putting a favourite toy just out of your baby's reach and watch her go for it!

A basketful of toys Babies have short attention spans so a large number of simple toys, rather than a few expensive ones, are preferable. Babies also enjoy putting objects into and taking them out of containers.

Interactive toys Once your child develops some dexterity she will enjoy shape sorters, pressing buttons, moving levers and imitating the actions of the adults around her.

Multi-use toys Many toys can be used in more than one way. Spools, for example, can be placed one on top of another or threaded on a string and pulled.

Make your own fun Something as simple as a piece of cloth or a feather can engage your baby's interest, and teach her about texture and pliability, as well as heightening her hand-eye coordination.

Hanging toys Many seats or mats incorporate bright, dangling toys. Your baby will be enticed by these and will want to reach towards them. They will 'exercise' her, at the same time as providing visual stimulation.

WE NEED TO TALK | ABOUT SPOILING

The busy lives we lead nowadays mean that we often resort to shortcuts to meet the needs of our children. This could be your partner buying regular treats and small toys to entertain your child while she gets on with some work, or you coming home with a huge teddy bear because you feel guilty for not spending enough time with your child. But your child may become ever more demanding and you will start to realise that you are 'spoiling' her. In these circumstances it's easy to forget that the most important gift you can give your child, and the one she will value most, is your time. You and your partner need to review what you are giving your child in terms of material gifts and quality time. Agree the limits and toughen up your regime, if necessary, so that treats really are treats. You may have to put up with extra tantrums at first but the long-term results will be worth it. Another good idea is to rotate your child's existing toys, putting some away and then reintroducing them after a month or so.

Protecting your baby

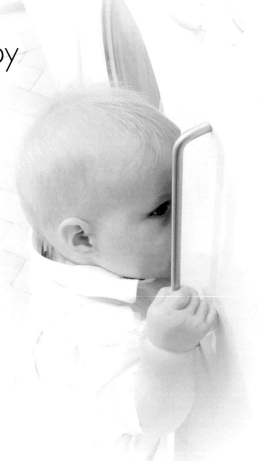

Until your baby starts crawling, safety in the home is probably not at the top of your list of priorities. But it is a good idea to address general safety issues as soon as possible. For example, it may now be time to finally install the smoke alarms that you have been planning for years.

As your baby starts to sit, roll, crawl, stand, walk and climb, at each stage you will need to completely rethink your strategies for safety in the home. The more you can do in advance of your child becoming mobile, and therefore needing constant attention, the better.

A general tip worth remembering is to be wary of chain reactions that can transform an apparently safe situation into one of danger. For example, a hot drink left in the centre of a kitchen table can become dangerous when your baby grabs the trailing edge of the tablecloth and pulls hard.

David's story

It was three days before her christening and I was sitting on the couch at home speaking on the telephone to the minister, checking the final details of the ceremony. My daughter was six months old and not yet crawling but could roll herself around. She was asleep on the couch next to me. While I was talking she woke up and rolled over the edge of the couch, landing head first on the wooden floor. I was horrified and picked her up to see an egg-shaped bump growing rapidly on her forehead. Fortunately our doctor's surgery was only a few minutes away and I rushed up there. By the time we saw the doctor my daughter seemed fine, though still had the lump. The doctor asked me whether she had been unconscious or had vomited, and whether I had been able to distract her from crying with anything that would usually catch her attention. The answers were no, no, yes. Suddenly it didn't seem so serious. He said we should monitor her overnight but there was unlikely to be any problems. It was good that the bump showed up – better on the outside of the skull than inside, he said. When I told my wife what had happened she took it in her stride. She was far more accustomed to the daily bumps and bruises of a baby's life. Having said that, she was less than happy that the accident was immortalised in our daughter's christening photographs.

It's not just crawling babies who turn your home into a minefield. Many children will roll before they can crawl, and will do so surprisingly quickly with a bit of practice. This means that they can roll into things such as table legs and destabilise them, knocking heavy items down onto themselves. They also are quick to pull on electric wires and repeatedly jam their fingers into plug sockets. Of course it's virtually impossible to keep floors tidy with a baby around, and he will always find the one object small enough to choke on and cram it in to his mouth. Scraps of food are also quickly eaten up, each carrying just enough harmful bacteria to cause a stomach upset. Small, hard objects left lying on the floor can be very painful when a baby rolls his ribcage over them. While rolling, he is bound to bash his head onto furniture or fittings at floor level, and probably burn himself as well when he rolls against the bottom end of a radiator. But, of course, the real danger comes when he spots the open stairway and starts rolling towards it ...

All of the hazards that come into play when your baby starts rolling, also apply to the crawling baby, except that the crawler is stronger, faster and can reach higher. Crawling babies require constant vigilance from an adult until they learn to walk. From then on, they need the constant vigilance of two adults.

Choosing and fitting a stair gate

If you have stairs in your home, then a gate is essential at the top and bottom. You will start by valiantly trying to find one that matches your décor, fail and finally end up with the cheapest. This is not a problem because they all do the same job. The problems start when you try to fit the gate. This is virtually impossible, so make sure you set aside several hours. If you go for the 'easy' option of a gate that holds itself in position with springs, the downside is that the bar that runs across the bottom of the frame will trip you up every time you walk through it. A good alternative to the traditional metal or wooden gate is the fabric, roller-blind style gate, which is very versatile and strong, though can be awkward to open and close. Good luck!

Tables Check tables to ensure they are stable and avoid using tablecloths, which can be pulled off by your baby.

Fires Use a fireguard, preferably one that does not get hot.

Hard floors Soften these with non-slip rugs. Check for exposed nails and splinters.

Kitchen Ideally, keep your baby out of the kitchen. As a precaution, check what your baby could reach. Attach child locks to cupboards and drawers or remove dangerous items.

Doorways Check where your baby is before opening or closing a door. If you want to keep a door open, use a doorstop to hold it in place.

Stairs You need a safety gate to stop your baby climbing up, as well as tumbling down, your stairs.

Plants Many common house and garden plants are poisonous. Babies will also eat the soil and push over pots.

Toilets Keep toilets clean, the toilet brush out of reach and, ideally, leave the bathroom door closed.

5

How do I cope with crying?

Understanding crying

Before your partner became pregnant (if you can remember that far back), probably the first thing you thought of when anyone mentioned babies was the sound of crying. It was that infernal noise you knew so well from irritating infants and inconsiderate parents who conspired to create those blood-curdling screeches on public transport, in restaurants and stores, and at those awful family gatherings you look forward to each year.

Looking back, perhaps you could have shown a little more understanding? The baby probably had a good reason for crying; maybe she had been hungry, in pain or bored. The parents would certainly have felt like crying, because they had probably tried everything they could think of to calm their baby. It may have been painful for you to listen to, but at least you could just walk away. Not any more.

Why do babies cry?

The average baby cries for a total of about one hour in every 24, for a variety of different reasons, throughout the day and night. Often, the periods of crying will change, so it may feel at times that your baby is crying more than previously, whereas in fact she's crying for the same period of time overall, it's just a new pattern.

Crying is a baby's main method of communication. It's not her only way of communicating, because she already has elements of body language and a range of facial expressions to subtly indicate her feelings and needs. But there is nothing subtle about a crying baby. Your baby's cry is nature's way of ensuring that she gets what she needs to survive. She's asking for something. It could be that she needs food, a drink, some pain relief, or someone to play with her. What she's certainly not doing is trying to annoy you. She's just

NO APPARENT REASON?

Most babies go through a fussy period every day (often at the same time each day) when nothing you do seems to help. Things to try are playing quiet music, a quick outing in the fresh air or a drive in the car. If your baby cries inconsolably in the early evening and she is beween three and 14 weeks old, she may be suffering from colic. If you don't think it's colic, and nothing you do 'works', you should express your concerns to your doctor or health visitor.

doing what her body is telling her is necessary. Some people will dismiss a baby's cries as 'attention seeking'. But how else can a baby address her needs, even if it is 'just' boredom or loneliness, without seeking the attention of her parent? An adult who is bored or lonely will try to do something about it – why not your baby?

So there's no getting away from the fact that your baby will spend a reasonable amount of time crying every day. The best way to lessen the impact on the sanity of your household is to try to 'tune in' to your baby as an individual. After a while, you should be able to recognise the different types of cry that your baby makes when she needs different things. For example, a shrill cry would suggest pain, while a low, grumbling cry probably means that she's bored. The quicker that you can recognise what she's asking for, the sooner you can meet her need and end the crying.

Of course, it's even better if you can learn to predict her needs before she starts crying, by getting to know how she will react to certain situations and stimulants, observing her daily patterns of behaviour, or by recognising her body language as she builds up to another bout of tears.

The curse of colic

It's bad enough that your newborn baby needs to cry for an hour a day. But what if she was to cry for at least three hours a day, for three or more days a week, over a period of three weeks or more? That's the official definition of colic for otherwise well-fed and healthy babies. This mysterious condition has no known cause or proven cure but affects between 10-20 per cent of babies and can drive parents to distraction.

Many theories have been put forward but none has pinpointed a single cause, and it may well be that there are a variety of different factors that prompt the daily, prolonged bouts of crying. The precise definition of colic, as set down in the 1950s, refers to periods of irritability, fussing and crying. Usually these take place during the late afternoon and early evening, just when everyone is feeling tired and stressed and the household is preparing for dinner and bed.

If you are at work all day and your partner is caring for your baby, then clearly she is going to need a lot of extra support. Do whatever you can to ensure she gets as much sleep as possible; look after your baby at the weekends so your partner can get out of the house, make sure she has friends and family to meet or talk to during the day, hire a babysitter to ease the pressure, and take time off work whenever the situation seems particularly bad.

The light at the end of the tunnel is that colic usually ends within three months of birth, often abruptly. For those who have to suffer it, not least the baby, it's a very tough time. But colic has no long-term adverse effects on the child and there is an upside in that it can bring a family closer together. Certainly you develop an in-depth understanding of your baby's individual needs, having invested so much time in trying to find out why she is distressed. And your child may actually benefit developmentally from all the extra love and attention she has received during this otherwise painful period.

Paul's story

Our daughter has suffered from colic pretty much since the day she took her first feed and usually cries for three hours a day, in the late afternoon or early evening. She has just turned 6 months – which I have been advised by many books, parents and childcare nurses, is the watershed time for her to suddenly stop crying. Unfortunately, nobody has made this clear to her.

Colic results in a lot of pain – I'm talking about me. I've tried the deep voice treatment, the stern male tone to bring her to a sudden realisation that I am the boss, but this only works for a split second as she gives me a quizzical look and then gets back to the crying with extra volume. She seems to be able to find just the right pitch for maximum discomfort, especially when I need to get up early for work or am trying to watch my favourite TV programme. At least I'm managing to keep my sense of humour... so far.

POSSIBLE CAUSES OF PERSISTENT CRYING

Colic usually starts within two weeks of birth, and a wide range of potential causes have been identified, though none proven. Once you have ruled out all the usual reasons why your baby cries, work through the following list to see if anything arouses your suspicions. Many of these conditions will require the advice of a doctor before attempting to ease the symptoms, and it's always a good idea to seek medical advice just in case the crying is a result of a serious underlying illness.

Immature digestive system One theory is that this part of your baby's internal system has not yet fully developed, resulting in abdominal pain. A colicky baby will often pull up her knees to her stomach when crying.

Immature nervous system Another suggestion is that your baby's nervous system is still developing and she cannot yet cope with loud noises, bright lights, or even the general stresses and sounds of home life going on around her.

Cow's milk Some babies are found to be intolerant of cow's milk and related products, such as cheese. This can even affect them when delivered through breastmilk after their mothers have consumed the product.

Infection Your baby may well be suffering from thrush, a cold or an ear infection, for example, which is causing her pain or discomfort.

Antenatal problems Some babies are born with hernias, others with dislocated hips. The squeezing of the baby's head during birth also can lead to painful skull problems.

Lactose overload When a baby is not latching onto the breast properly this can lead to overfeeding. The excess lactose that she takes in through the milk eventually passes into the gut, drawing in fluids and causing bacteria to ferment, in turn leading to gas, loose stools and stomach ache.

Stress on the pregnant mother Research has shown that babies whose mothers are stressed by traumatic events during pregnancy, can be more likely to suffer colic once they are born.

Difficult birth A problematic vaginal birth, for example, one which required a forceps delivery, is often cited as a reason for a baby crying more and sleeping less than others. Babies born by Caesarean section generally seem more relaxed, not having experienced the squeeze through the birth canal.

John's story

I've always found that singing songs is a great way of calming my children, especially when they wake up crying at night or I'm having trouble getting them to sleep. I don't actually know any official lullabies so had to dredge my childhood memories for hymns and nursery rhymes with my first baby. 'Away in a manger' was the only song I knew all the words to, but it didn't seem to matter because babies love repetition – hearing something they recognise makes them feel secure. Often it would only take the first word of the song to stop my son crying. It was as if I had the password that he needed to hear before he could relax again and go back to sleep.

Soothing your crying baby

It's important that you respond to your young baby's cries within a few minutes. The longer you leave her to cry, the more distressed she will become, making it more difficult to interpret the original source of her anxiety. There are many reasons why a baby may feel the need to cry, just as we experience a huge range of feelings and stimulants that prompt us to behave in the way that we do.

Babies whose cries are ignored become non–responsive as they mature. You will not be spoiling your baby by acting on her cries, but you will be communicating to her that her needs are important to you and that they will be met.

Controlling your emotions

This is the difficult part. How do you keep your cool when everything around you seems to be in meltdown? Your partner is exhausted and tearful after a long, hard day looking after your baby. You are almost asleep on your feet having slept badly the previous night, and it was a tough day at the office. You are now trying to put your daughter to bed but she just will not go to sleep. You're walking her around the room singing songs to her but every time she appears to nod off, and you lean over to lay her in her cot, she wakes up again and starts crying. You begin to feel that she's deliberately trying to make you angry – and it's working. Of course your baby is not consciously trying to make your life difficult, she's probably just asking for help to go to sleep. And deep down you know that, but right now it doesn't matter.

There's no escaping the fact that your baby's behaviour will make you, and your partner, very angry at times. But it's a natural response and there's no shame in feeling that way, or having violent feelings, as long as you are able to control your emotions and direct your anger away from your child.

The first thing to do is acknowledge your anger, because it's only then that you can deal with it constructively. Once you have worked out specifically what it is that triggers an angry reaction, and when it is most likely to happen, you can develop coping strategies and put them into action.

Essentially, when you are confronted with a provocative situation, you need to find a mental or physical means of releasing the growing tension within you before it generates an explosion. Ideally, you will have thought about these mechanisms in advance, so that you can switch to a completely different mental or physical focus as soon as you feel the need. For example, before you take your baby to bed, have in your mind an issue that is bothering you from a completely unrelated part of your life, that you can switch your thoughts to and help shut out the sound of crying. Alternatively, pick a favourite song to sing – out loud or in your head – and take to the stage when the going gets tough.

To physically relieve the tension, you could punch a cushion, or step outside the room and do some exercises, or simply walk away for a few minutes.

You could also try some relaxation techniques. For example, stand up straight and take a deep breath. Breathe out, in one long breath, until you feel that you have no breath left inside you. Slowly drop your shoulders as the breath leaves your body. Then, without breathing in, breathe out again, further dropping your shoulders, until you really feel that your lungs are empty. Repeat this exercise a few times and you should feel the tension drain away from your upper body.

The key thing about controlling your emotions is to clear your mind after each stressful event. If your anger is left to fester, the next time you have to deal with a difficult situation, your stress levels will already be dangerously high. So if your daughter is waking

■ **TOP TIPS See the funny side**

The key to controlling your emotions is to be able to switch your thoughts to something completely different before you lose control. Your sense of humour can provide an instant cure in difficult situations.

Tell yourself a joke Always have ready a favourite joke or your funniest film scene, or the most hilarious thing that has ever happened to you, so that you can tune into it when the going gets tough and completely alter your mood.

Pull a funny face You know, of course, that your baby is not your enemy, but when her behaviour is really starting to irritate, imagine yourself back at school and pull funny faces at her. This is a piece of harmless fun that breaks the tension and is surprisingly therapeutic – who knows, the trick may even raise a laugh from your child!

up every hour throughout the evening, plan something that you know will definitely relieve the pressure in each period between visits to her bedroom. And make sure that you arrange your evening meal to be ready to eat immediately after one of her waking episodes, so that you don't sit down with your dinner an hour later just as the crying starts again.

6

Sleep issues

Bed and your baby

Life used to be so different. In the days before nappies and bottles, you could pretty much take sleep for granted. You could stay up as late as you wanted to, safe in the knowledge that you would catch up the following night or at the weekend. And, of course, you had the luxury of lying-in on Saturdays and Sundays, taking breakfast in bed, watching television, reading the weekend newspapers, or just dozing. Was it all just a dream?

Now sleep is a valuable commodity and you have to trade hours with your partner in the vain hope of getting enough to function as a normal human being. You fall asleep at the slightest opportunity, in the most awkward positions, so that even sitting on the toilet is a chance for catching up – until you're woken by your partner hammering on the door, accusing you of 'hiding'.

Fear not. The sleep situation should improve after the first three months, when your baby settles into more of a routine. And until then your lack of sleep is a great ice-breaker when meeting other new mums and dads.

Choosing your baby a bed

Until he has a regular night-time routine, you will be able to take your baby out with you in the evenings, so a first bed could be something portable like a Moses basket. Make sure your basket has a strong, wide base, that there are no sharp edges and it is fitted with a firm mattress that fits snugly against the sides.

If you're buying a cot, don't buy a second-hand one, because you won't know its history. Choose one where the gaps in the side rails are no more than 8 cm wide and ensure that it comes with a close-fitting mattress. Other important features are dual releases on the side rails, well-assembled joints and mechanisms, and a plain, practical design. Avoid those with cut-

SUDDEN INFANT DEATH SYNDROME

Also known as cot death, SIDS is every parent's nightmare, but recent research has led to a better understanding of the risks and preventative measures.

Most important is that your baby should always be put down to sleep on his back, with his feet touching the foot of his cot. Another important risk factor is smoking – both during and after pregnancy. Exposure to one parent's smoke doubles the risk of a baby dying of SIDS. Don't let anyone smoke in the same room as your baby and don't burn incense in your baby's room. Make sure the room is sufficiently heated – between 16° and 20° C – and use several light blankets instead of a single heavy one. Avoid insulators like cot bumpers, sheepskins and duvets. Don't cover your baby's head or put a pillow in the cot.

outs. If you've been given a cot, you will need to buy a new mattress. The mattress should be firm, plastic- covered and with reinforced corners and sides. If you're buying a foam mattress, make sure it's a high density one – about 24 kg per cubic metre – which has ventilated sections at the top and in the middle. If you're choosing a sprung mattress, look for one with a minimum of 150 coils.

Helping with night-time feeding

It may seem at first that one of the great benefits of breastfeeding is that only the woman can do it, thereby exempting the father from all night-time feeding duties. But how many women are going to allow their partners to opt out of all responsibility for the baby once the lights go out? And you would also be missing out on another valuable bonding opportunity with your baby.

Even if your baby is being wholly breastfed, you can still be a big help simply by being first out of bed to pick him up from his cot when he starts crying. You can give him a cuddle and a few words of comfort while your partner gets herself into a comfortable feeding position.

If your partner feeds your baby in bed, have a lamp set up at her side so that she can read to help pass the time, but keep the light dim so as not to disturb your baby. Check that she has everything she needs for her own comfort, as well as nappy changing kit and other essential baby items – though of course you could always take charge of nappy changing during the night. Breastfeeding is thirsty work so make sure there is plenty of drinking water available and maybe she would like a hot drink to start with? Does she have enough easy reading material? Look out for her favourite magazines while you're shopping to keep her selection topped up.

After about six weeks of breastfeeding the mother-baby bond should be properly established and you can start to give your baby the occasional bottle, including a night-time feed. If your baby is totally bottlefed then you really have no excuse for avoiding the night shift! Even if your partner decides that she will do the majority of night-time feeds, you can still help by preparing the formula milk and bottles beforehand, as well as warming them when needed.

Maximising your sleep

Your baby will need to sleep in your bedroom for at least the first six weeks after birth, so that you can respond quickly to his cries and ensure that he does not feel insecure or abandoned. Inevitably you will have to wake up during the night to help comfort him, but you may not have bargained for the noises that he makes while sleeping, such as the snuffles, coughs, heavy breathing and occasional shrieks, that can also cut in to your sleep time. Then there are the slurping noises that accompany any feeding that takes place in the early hours, which can seem to be hugely amplified in the quiet of the night when you are already irritable and finding it difficult to get back to sleep.

The chances are that your partner will push herself extremely hard to meet your baby's needs, and no matter how exhausted she feels,

---

LAYING BABY DOWN TO SLEEP

1 Gently ease your baby away from your body. From a cradling position, gently slide your arms apart so that one hand supports your baby's head and neck, while the other supports his bottom. Slowly move him away from your body and over a padded surface.

2 Lower your baby down. Turn your baby's body so that it is in line with your own. Bend close to the changing mat or mattress and slowly lower him onto the surface, putting his bottom down first.

3 Remove your hands. Once he has made contact with the surface, gently ease your supporting hand from underneath his bottom, then lower his upper body and head. Keep his head well supported until it is resting comfortably on the surface, before gently sliding your hand away.

The jury is still out on whether it's a good idea for babies to sleep in a bed with their parents. There are said to be advantages in that your baby feels more confident and secure, while the three of you develop a strong bond as a family unit. But there are also clear dangers and you should follow the official guidance closely if you decide to share a bed with your baby:

- Do not do so if you are extremely tired, or have used alcohol or drugs to the point where you will not easily wake up.
- Do not place your baby under a heavy quilt or covers, under which he could slip and be smothered.
- Do not place your baby on top of soft bedding material that he could roll over on and suffocate.
- Your partner should only breastfeed in a position that prevents her from falling asleep on top of your baby.

about three or four months old, and some much older. However, bottlefed babies may start sleeping for this long at an even earlier age.

Having said that, it is important to establish a bedtime routine, lasting no more than 45 minutes to an hour in the early weeks. This will gradually help your baby recognise the various cues for going to sleep. Some things to try are giving him a bath to calm him down and dressing him in different clothes at bedtime. Feed him in a dimly lit and quiet room and give him a cuddle. If you can, leave the room and let him settle himself down to sleep, but don't expect this to work every time!

If your baby wakes up and cries in the night, it's probably because he needs something (see page 60) although some parents believe that if they always go in when their baby cries in the night, he will never learn to sleep through. When you do go into your baby, try to sort out the problem without picking him up or putting on the light. Stroke him gently and talk to him quietly before tiptoeing out again.

she will still try to fit in other household chores as well. Do everything you can to encourage her to take naps during the day when your baby is asleep, or when you are there to cover for her. If she says she's not tired, suggest that she lies down on the bed and closes her eyes – if she doesn't fall asleep, then she's not tired.

These naps are important not only for her sake but also because it means that she will be better able to cope with the night-time duties and relieve the pressure on you. That may sound selfish but actually it's just good teamwork.

Sleeping through the night

For most babies, sleeping through the night means sleeping for a five-hour stretch. The majority of babies do not begin to establish this sort of regular sleeping pattern until they are

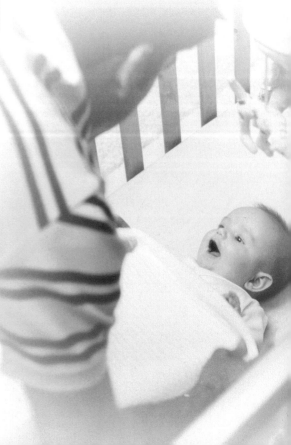

7

Out and about

Travelling with your baby

It's never too soon to include your baby in your outings, as long as you take certain precautions. It's a good idea to avoid crowds and rush hours when you could be jostled, and also aim to avoid people who might be ill.

There is no special age that your baby needs to be before you can take her outside, as long as you are well prepared and your baby is properly dressed. Your young baby cannot fully regulate her body temperature so always dress her in one more layer of clothing than you would wear in the same environment, and check her frequently to make sure she's not cold or hot.

It's best not to skimp on the essential carrying and travelling gear, because high quality goods should make your life a lot easier when transporting your baby, and will hopefully last for another child. Buying second-hand items such as car seats can be a risk in terms of child safety, though friends and family are a good source if you know the history of the item and, of course, trust their judgment!

There are always innovative new products and designs coming on to the market, so once you think you know what you need, do some thorough research and seek the advice of specialist retailers and other parents before making a purchase.

Baby carriers and backpacks

These enable you to keep your baby close but your hands free. Baby carriers are sold according to the child's age or weight and most allow you to hold your baby either close to your chest or facing outwards. Make sure you choose one that fits you comfortably and holds your baby securely. Wide, well-padded shoulder and back straps will help to distribute her weight evenly, and there should be stiff padding to support her head and neck. See the box, opposite, for advice on using a carrier.

Backpacks for older babies are basically open-topped rucksacks, specially designed to include a seat within the frame. Your baby can sit high up and watch the world go by from an interesting new vantage point. This makes walking in the countryside easier because you no longer have to worry about struggling down rough tracks with the pushchair. As long as you buy one of good quality, the backpack should be comfortable to wear, and will certainly aid your upper body development – especially as some backpacks will accommodate children of

PUTTING ON A BABY CARRIER

Follow the manufacturer's instructions to fasten the straps and buckles. When you feel comfortable and the carrier is secure, pick up your baby. Sit down comfortably on a chair and open out the carrier. Holding your baby under her armpits, slowly lift her into the carrier. Once she's comfortably seated, check that your baby's weight is evenly supported and adjust the straps accordingly. When you are ready to take your baby out of the carrier, make sure you are both in a safe place first. As before, sit down in a chair; loosen the straps then lean forwards as you lift your baby out. Lay her down in her cot or on a changing mat and then remove the carrier.

up to 22kg! Make sure that yours has a sun shade because your baby will get extra exposure up there. A handheld mirror can be used to check on what your baby is doing.

Choosing a pushchair

Your pushchair will be one of the most important purchases you and your partner will make because it will go everywhere with you for the foreseeable future. So choose one that fits your physiques and lifestyle, as well as the needs of your baby.

The first thing to check is that your newborn can comfortably lie flat in the pushchair. This is a must, because sitting up for too long will damage her developing spine.

Your comfort also needs to be considered, so the height and positioning of the handle is important, as well as the weight and manoeuvrability of the pushchair. If you live in an area with bumpy paths or lots of hills, then you may want to consider air-filled rather than solid tyres, though you will also need to invest in a puncture repair kit. Check how easy it is to fold up the chair, especially if you plan to use public transport. Will it fit in to the boot of your car, or through the front door of your home? Where will you store it when it's not in use? The important point is to shop around, ask to see demonstrations and get a hands-on feel for each pushchair.

Car travel

You will need to buy several car seats over the first few years of your child's life, and choosing correctly is vital from a safety point of view.

There are legal standards that all manufactures have to meet, so the difficult part for you is finding the seat that best fits your car. It has to fit snugly in to the seat with minimal sideways movement, but be easy to lift in and out. As with choosing your pushchair, a demonstration is always helpful, and some stores will actually fit the chair for you.

If your baby is born in hospital you will need a car seat to bring her home. This first purchase will be a rear-facing, portable car seat that can be removed from the car and used as a carrier, chair or rocker, or one that comes as part of a pushchair carry system. Babies should ride in these rear-facing seats for as long as possible, and at least until the age of 9-12 months. Infant car seats are best placed on the back seat, but wherever you use them make sure there is no airbag fitted because they can smother your baby if activated.

A young baby should not spend long periods scrunched up asleep in her first travel seat, but a carry seat is great for a lunchtime nap in the car or for whisking your baby into a restaurant, and then back again before she wakes up!

When your baby is about nine months old you will need a new car seat. This one will be forward-facing and should take her up to her fourth birthday. The best way to decide whether your child is ready for a switch is to compare your baby's weight against the manufacturer's instructions.

Feeding on the move

One of the many benefits of breastfeeding is that it's much easier to feed your baby when travelling, compared to the extra equipment and hassle

YOUR ESSENTIAL TRAVEL KIT
- Changing mat, nappies, nappy sacs
- Nappy wipes
- Sunscreen lotion in warm weather
- Bottle/carton of formula milk (if baby is not being breastfed)
- Water or juice in a bottle (for older babies)
- Baby food, bowl, spoon and bib (if weaning)
- Change of clothes
- Hat. In summer, one with a wide brim to protect against sunburn; in winter a warm one to prevent heat loss.

required to feed your baby by bottle. Your partner's milk is always ready, and always at the right temperature. And the comfort of nursing can reduce the stress on your baby of being in different places. Often your baby will sleep throughout a journey, so try to travel in time with her usual naps and make the most it.

WE NEED TO TALK | ABOUT MANAGEABLE OUTINGS

By the time you reach the weekend, you and your partner will have lots of errands to cram into those precious two days, and you may also be keen to give your baby the best possible day out – as well as find some relaxation time for yourselves. So it's easy to fall into the trap of trying to do too much. Babies and young children can quickly become over-stimulated, and a day packed with visits, shopping and car trips, will be tiring for all of you. Everything seems important, or great fun, but take a few minutes to sit down together and review your plans. Count up how many times you will get in and out of the car, for example, how many people you'll meet and roughly how many destinations you'll visit. What sounded perfectly manageable to start with, may now look like an arduous marathon.

8

My older baby

Toddlers – a different ball game

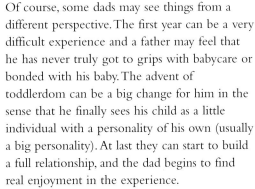

It usually takes about a year after the birth until you finally feel that you've cracked the babycare game. You've mastered the arts of nappy changing and feeding, you feel a solid bond with your child, the relationship with your partner is better than ever, and you've even learned to cope with your new waking hours. Just as you begin to enjoy this feeling of contentment, everything changes.

Suddenly, your baby has transformed into a toddler. You had marvelled at his first steps, his new facial expressions and his garbled attempts at language, now these various, seemingly unlinked, aspects of his development have joined forces to create a little ball of energy that just will not stop bouncing. Indeed, it's a whole new ball game.

Of course, some dads may see things from a different perspective. The first year can be a very difficult experience and a father may feel that he has never truly got to grips with babycare or bonded with his baby. The advent of toddlerdom can be a big change for him in the sense that he finally sees his child as a little individual with a personality of his own (usually a big personality). At last they can start to build a full relationship, and the dad begins to find real enjoyment in the experience.

Either way, this period is a major turning point for dads. A toddler can do all sorts of things that a baby could never do, such as walking, talking, climbing, and saying 'no'. He also will have the rudimentary skills necessary to play football, which opens up a whole new range of football-related activities that had hitherto lain dormant, including the joy of watching football on television, albeit for very short periods. This is also a time when even girls can be introduced to football kits and chased around the garden with a ball, before their mothers teach them the phrase 'Daddy, this is boring.'

So there is a great deal of extra fun that can be had with toddlers, and dads can enjoy a new sense of fulfilment if they take advantage of the opportunities to become more involved in their lives. There are also, of course, many new challenges. At the most basic level, you will need to review the safety of your home to cope with a more active, able, inquisitive child. But as well as his physical development, there are also the more challenging emotional changes that your toddler will be facing over the next couple of years, as his character really starts to develop. He will be constantly learning and often feel tired and grouchy but will probably never want to go to sleep – unless, of course, it's a particularly inconvenient time for you. This is when some parents come to feel that they've created a monster, and they just hope they can survive until the child starts school!

In truth, it's not just the change from baby to toddler, but the series of changes throughout his time as a toddler, that is so challenging for his parents. There is always an issue to address or a habit to break, whether it's potty training or trying to keep him out of your bed at night. And then months after you think you've solved one problem, it will suddenly reappear.

But despite all the battles, this is the time when you fall hopelessly in love with your child. At each stage of toddlerdom you think 'This is a wonderful age', and you're sure that it will never be bettered. Then your child changes and you grow used to this new child and start to think 'Actually, this is the best age'. Then he changes again, and so on. The only real sadness is that each new era signals the end of the previous, and you will soon start to feel that your child is simply growing up too fast – which is all the more reason to enjoy this period while it lasts.

WE NEED TO TALK | ABOUT WEEKENDS

Saturdays can be a nightmare. You would think that to spend the whole day as a family would be happiness itself. But while you may be happy to relax at home with your toddler, your partner has been climbing the walls all week and now you are cluttering up the place and ruining her routines. There are only two solutions and both involve you spending quality, one-on-one time with your child: either you and your child go out, or your partner goes out. Actually there's a third option – you go out and then she goes out as you come back in. If you take your child out and your partner stays at home, she will probably want to catch up with chores instead of relaxing. This can be very frustrating for you. But if she catches up and then has the chance to go out with friends, or take a course, or go shopping, then she is more likely to properly relax and you can really start to enjoy the weekend together as a family. So it's up to you to take the initiative.

Pete's story

It must be a tough job being a toddler. They have loads of fun but so much is expected of them. Because they're so good at copying us, and they even dress like us, we start to think of them as little adults. I found it so frustrating that most of the time my son was like a mini version of me, but then I couldn't make him understand what seemed like really simple ideas. And when he was tired or frustrated he would burst in to tears, or just throw a tantrum for no reason. Eventually, it dawned on me that, actually, he was still a baby and I had to give up my adult expectations of him and just go with the flow.

Meeting your toddler's needs

The toddler is a complex beast but there are essentially three areas that require attention from you to enable your child to thrive: nutritional needs, emotional needs and recreational needs. Of course, your toddler does not have a copy of this list so it can be extremely difficult to ensure she fulfils all the requirements on a daily basis. While it's good to have guidelines, for example on what she should eat every day, you have to be realistic and take the broad view that as long you are aware of her essential needs, and are meeting them over a period of time, then at least you are on the right track.

Nutritional needs

Combining good nutrition with healthy eating habits during the toddler years will help lay the foundations for future good health. A balanced diet ensures that your child has sufficient

If your child regularly eats something from each of the main food groups, then she is likely to get all the nutrients (protein, carbohydrate, fat, vitamins and minerals) she requires for good health.

Meat and meat alternatives Aim for one meat, fish or egg serving daily, or two from plant sources such as pulses or beans.

Dairy products Aim for at least 350 ml (½ pint) full-fat milk daily or two servings of cheese, fromage frais or yoghurt.

Fruit and vegetables Aim for at least five servings daily of fresh, tinned or frozen fruit and vegetables. Fruit juice should count as only one serving even if given more than once.

Grain products and starchy foods Aim for at least one serving each mealtime of bread, corn, rice, cereal or starchy vegetables. Avoid very rough grains.

Fat and sugar A balanced diet should provide sufficient amounts of these. Refined sugars and processed fats should be avoided.

nutrition for energy and growth, while protecting her against illness and promoting mental development.

But a healthy diet for toddlers is not necessarily the same as for adults. Toddlers have very high daily requirements for energy (calories) and other nutrients, particularly after they begin to walk and become more active. However, because their stomachs are small, toddlers cannot eat large amounts of food at one sitting – a toddler-sized portion is usually about a third to half that of an adult. So ideally, your child should have three main meals a day with healthy snacks in between, eating easily digestible and nutrient-rich food from the five main food groups.

Emotional needs

The overriding theme of the toddler years is that of a journey from dependence to independence. Your child is developing from a baby who needs you to do everything for her, to an individual who will actively challenge your decisions and involvement in her life. She is taking major steps towards the character she will become as an adult, and being confronted with huge amounts of information about the world and relationships. She will feel and express emotions that she has never fully experienced before, and will need a father who can respond appropriately with comfort or discipline to her developing emotional needs.

Encouraging independence

To encourage your child to become more independent it's important to build up her self-confidence from an early age. Give her lots of love and attention and use positive reinforcement whenever she achieves something. Never make her feel like a failure for her inability to achieve something because

SAFETY FIRST WITH FOODS

- Avoid boiled sweets, whole nuts (especially peanuts) and whole grapes because of the risk of choking. Remove stones from peaches and nectarines.
- Don't give tea, coffee, squash or fizzy drinks. The former contain caffeine and the latter too much sugar, artificial flavourings, preservatives and colouring. Drinks with sweeteners can act as a laxative and give your child diarrhoea. Water or milk is best between meals; fruit juice should be offered with or after a meal and always from a cup not a bottle.
- Don't add salt to your child's food and limit crisps and other salty food. Too much salt can lead to your child having high blood pressure later in life.

she may become reluctant to try again. Engaging in a range of different activities and social situations will provide the stimulation and opportunity to try new things and develop her skills, helping her to be more confident in herself.

There are many daily routines, such as getting dressed, which provide opportunities to increase her independence, at the same time enhancing her physical and intellectual skills.

Allow her to make choices for herself, even if she makes mistakes at first. Avoid being dominant and always taking the lead when you play with her. Make deliberate mistakes when playing and allow her to correct you. Include her in adult conversations and encourage her to discuss her thoughts and feelings. These are all good ways of developing her self-confidence.

Recreational needs

One of the most important ways that your child learns to develop and practise her skills is through play. While providing mental, physical and social stimulation, it also increases your child's powers of observation and concentration.

Giving your child different types of toys and objects to play with teaches her about different shapes, sizes and textures, while helping her to develop self-expression and hand-eye co-ordination, and stimulating her creativity and imagination.

How your child plays

Aged 15-18 months
Your child will be curious about everything and desperate to explore, so it's a good idea to fill up a big box of household items for her to rummage through, and picture books for her to point out items that she recognises. All sorts of containers are fun, as are simple puzzles, crayons, and miniature versions of things that she sees mummy and daddy using, such as a dustpan and brush. She needs to practise her walking skills, so toys that she can stand up for pushing and pulling will also be well-used.

Aged two years
Her locomotive skills are now becoming more advanced and she will enjoy kicking and throwing balls, building blocks and imaginative play. Musical games, talking toys, tea sets and sandpits, are all favourites at this stage of her development.

Aged three years
Your child is now much better at controlling her hand movements, and will love playing with construction sets, looking at books and putting together jigsaw puzzles. Playing with sand, water, dough and paint will all help encourage exploration, co-ordination and creativity. Making a cake can be great fun, too – up to a point!

What your toddler can do

Toddlers are full of surprises. Just when you think you have the measure of your two-year-old, he'll suddenly add another dozen words to his vocabulary or complete a task that he could not even have attempted a few days before. At this stage a toddler really starts to reach out to the world, picking up information from all sorts of influences, and you often find yourself asking 'where did he learn that?' Sometimes you get the feeling that a big change is on its way. He seems to be on the verge of something new without actually trying to do it. He's thinking about it and storing up knowledge, which he finally unleashes and you see a flurry of developments in quick succession – much the same as a physical growth spurt.

Obviously, it's great if you can be around your child to experience these steps with him, but because that's not always possible, there are many ways that you can be involved and help to promote different aspects of your child's development.

The stages that he goes through on the path to becoming an independent person, capable of confident movement and fluid communication, are known as developmental milestones. As long as they are healthy and living in a nurturing environment, most children will reach these milestones by specific ages. But don't be disheartened or frustrated if your child is not 'hitting the targets'. These milestones act as a guide, but there is a wide variety in rates of development. You can help your child develop to his full potential but it's best not to compare him to other children. While children can vary in what they achieve when, the majority will be developing perfectly normally within the accepted ranges.

This chapter focuses on two key areas: physical development, which includes locomotive and manipulative skills; and mental development, which covers the ability to think and communicate. The important skills of social development, learning to relate to and interact with others, are dealt with in chapter 10.

You have a big part to play in your child's physical and mental development, even if you only have a short time to give on your working days. Compared to your partner, you will naturally offer different attitudes and approaches to the games and tasks that encourage your child's development. When your child plays with you, he will probably learn to do things in different ways and develop extra skills than he might learn from his mother. At the very least, your child's learning will be inspired by a change of playmate and, of course, your relationship will benefit from the increased communication.

Intellectual development

Also known as mental development, this includes the mastery of communication skills, such as speech, reading, drawing and counting, using the imagination and remembering things. There are various ways that you can help to promote these aspects of your child's development, particularly language skills. And, of course, talking to your child is one of the most important things you can do for him.

Promoting language skills

Always look at your child when talking to him and use short, simple sentences. Listen to him when he is speaking and allow him to finish his sentences. Expand on the things he says, for example if he says 'door', you might say 'the door is open'. Encourage him to talk to his toys, and always try to describe sights and sounds to him when you're out and about. Look at books together and point out characters and familiar objects. But avoid subjecting him to a barrage of too much information and instead build quiet times into his day.

Manipulation skills

Hand-eye co-ordination is involved in a lot of these physical skills. As your child gains dexterity, he will be able to use his hands and fingers for activities such as building blocks, drawing, doing up buttons and using a spoon and fork. These skills have to be learned, so you need to give your child every opportunity to practice. It's another good reason for spending time with your toddler, playing and exploring together, building your relationship while he develops these essential skills.

Promoting manipulation

■ Show him how to unscrew lids, thread things onto string, pour water, and turn pages, etc.
■ Teach him how to do things for himself, such as using a spoon and taking his socks off.
■ Give him activity boards and toys that have lots of features for pressing, turning and spinning.
■ Provide him with building blocks and stacking toys.
■ Work together on puzzles, drawing and painting.

Milestones in intellectual development

15-18 months:
• Points to familiar objects when looking at books.
• Says six to 20 words, particularly 'No'.
• Understands simple questions and instructions, such as 'Where are your pyjamas?' or 'Give me your toy'.
• May know two or three body parts.
• Imitates your gestures.
• Repeats own name.

Two years:
• Uses 50 or more words and may be putting two or three words together.
• Understands longer instructions, such as 'Put the cup on the table'.
• Understands simple short stories and conversations.
• Uses pronouns such as 'me', 'you' and 'I'. Begins to ask questions.

Three years:
• Knows two or three colours and some shapes.
• Carries on a simple conversation and talks and seems to be continually asking questions, such as 'Where', 'What' and 'Why'?
• Now understands more complex instructions, such as 'Please go to your bedroom and fetch your pyjamas'.
• May be able to count up to 10.
• Will start understanding concepts such as 'today' and 'tomorrow'.
• Can remember some nursery rhymes.

Milestones in locomotive development

15-18 months:
- Walks alone.
- Kneels and crawls upstairs on all fours.
- Walks upstairs by holding on to the rail and putting both feet on each step.
- Squats down or bends over to pick up a toy without falling.
- Climbs furniture.
- Waves goodbye.

Two years:
- Runs
- Walks backwards.
- Kicks a ball without falling over.
- Walks on tiptoe.
- Walks up and down steps with two feet per stair.

Three years:
- Can stand on one leg and hop.
- Walks upstairs with one foot to each stair.
- May jump from bottom step.
- Can jump with two feet.
- Rides a tricycle with two feet on the pedals.
- Dances to music.

Milestones in manipulative development

15-18 months:
- Can build a tower of three bricks.
- Has started to scribble.
- Can put a cup to his mouth without spilling.
- Feeds himself with a spoon, without losing too much food.
- Takes off his socks.
- Can do simple puzzles.

Two years:
- Can turn door handles.
- Turns the pages of a book properly.
- Can put on gloves, shoes and socks.
- Threads beads, feathers, buttons and a zip.
- Can unscrew lids from jars.

Three years:
- Begins to dress and undress with help.
- Can build a tower of nine bricks.
- Draws circles and copies a cross if shown.
- Eats with a fork and spoon.
- Holds pen properly.
- Can pick up small objects.
- Using both hands, he can pour water from a jug in to a cup without too much spillage.

Dressing

Clothes and footwear

The chances are that your partner will take responsibility for buying most of your child's clothes, but it's important to take an interest and at least try to have a viewpoint on what she wears – if only to avoid the accusation of leaving yet another parenting task to your partner.

With toddlers you don't need to be too precious about their clothes. Obviously it's great to see your child looking good, and of course you like to see her well dressed for special occasions, but rest assured that your child will be doing her best to ruin or grow out of everything that you buy for her in as short a time as possible.

The key thing is that your child will be expending loads of energy in her clothes, so look for items that are easy to clean, hard wearing, loose fitting and breathable. And you will find it easier to dress your child for different weather and locations by choosing clothes that can be worn as layers, rather than buying huge, thick jumpers, for example, which have limited use.

To save money on children's clothes, think ahead and buy sale items in a bigger size so that your child can wear them the following year. There are also bargains to be had in the growing number of children's clothes agencies, which sell quality secondhand clothes on commission – and you could sell your nearly new baby clothes there as well. If you're really lucky, you'll have a friend or relative with a child slightly older than yours who grows out of her clothes just in time for your child to step into them.

Shoes

Once your child is walking outdoors and her feet need some protection, it's essential that she has a pair of correctly fitting shoes. There is little hard bone in a child's foot; it's basically cartilage and gristle, so that pressure from badly fitting shoes or socks can distort the shape of the foot and may cause permanent damage. And because there is so little bone in the foot, your child may not feel it hurting and will not complain. Your child's shoes should be fitted by a trained shoe fitter and never be bought secondhand or passed down from older siblings.

The type of shoe you buy should be of the correct size and width, and made of natural materials such as leather or canvas, which allow the foot to 'breathe'. The shoes should have plenty of room to grow at the toes, while the heel end should be snug-fitting and firm, to cradle the foot without restriction or slipping. Although sandals are cooler in the summer, their less robust construction means that they are more likely to harm your child's feet, and need to be professionally fitted.

Children's feet grow so quickly that there is little point buying expensive shoes. Shoes should be re-checked for fitting every two months, and your child will probably need a new pair every four to six months until she is five years old.

Whenever it's safe to do so, let your child walk barefoot to help her feet develop healthily.

Dressing your toddler

Have you ever heard an exasperated mum tell a friend: 'She was dressed by her father'? If not, then it's only a matter of time.

Most men, try as we might, do not have a great feeling for what looks good to wear. We spend most of our waking hours at work, where our dress is largely dictated by the type of job we do. When we are asleep it doesn't really matter what we wear, and in the short periods of leisure in between work and sleep, we essentially stick to what we know – those few items or styles that we have learnt through much trial and error will always work for us (we think). Even then, many of us will be directed by our partners and, if the age-old stereotype is correct that we hate shopping, our partners even may buy our clothes without consulting us.

So the thought of having to dress your child may be one that sends shivers down the spine. All of those carefully buried insecurities may come back to haunt you as you contemplate

WE NEED TO TALK | ABOUT HELPING WITH DRESSING

Your partner wants to do everything for your toddler because she is more practised and therefore quicker. This includes dressing the child, for which she also thinks she has natural flair. She is probably right in both of these assertions but dressing your own child can be fun and rewarding for dads, especially when it's not an everyday chore. It's a good bonding experience and you can really see your child developing over the months as she gradually learns to make her own decisions about clothing and starts to dress herself. And, of course, if you are never allowed to practice, how can you possibly improve? It's also a break for your partner, but approach it sensitively so that she doesn't feel her capabilities are being undermined.

Try to take the initiative every so often by going to the shops, or onto the internet, in your lunch break, and buy something for your child to wear. It doesn't have to be a full outfit, just a hat or a pair of fancy socks, which your daughter will love and your partner will appreciate. Also, keep an eye out for holes in tights and socks, or pants that are looking tight, and quietly top up your child's wardrobe before your partner needs to do it.

taking responsibility for dressing another human being. But it's actually not that difficult, and should be fun for you both. If you pay attention to detail, it soon becomes second nature. And if you do have a disaster, you can always blame the child for refusing to wear your perfect choices.

Making dressing easier

Learning to dress is an important part of your child's journey towards independence, so let her try to do it herself even though it can mean very slow progress. Don't expect too much at first, and avoid laughing or doing anything that might discourage her from trying. Try to be relaxed about her choice of colours, so that she can feel good about the job she's doing. Lay out a selection of suitable outfits and let her choose, making sure the clothes are easy to pick up and put on without her having to decide which is the front or back of the garment.

Problems with dressing

Some toddlers are so keen to dress themselves that they refuse all help, even when you are desperate to get them out of the house. While this is frustrating, it's best to allow as much time as possible for your enthusiastic toddler to dress herself, because you will see the benefits as soon as she learns to speed up.

At the other end of the spectrum, toddlers often can refuse to get dressed, or will take off their clothes afterwards. It can sometimes be impossible to get them dressed to go out.

One way of minimising arguments is to buy more of the clothes that your child likes, even if it means she has several items that are exactly the same. You can also limit the number of clothing options by only making certain items accessible at her level. Otherwise, you may just have to fight it out!

Fastenings

When your toddler is learning how to use a zip, teach her how to keep it away from her skin and clothes to prevent it catching. When she is being toilet-trained, make sure she has trousers with elasticated waists that are easy to pull up and down. Teach her to button her clothes from the bottom upwards, so that she fits them into the correct holes.

Eating

Having regularly returned from work to find your toddler drenched in pasta sauce, probably the last thing you can imagine doing is sitting down for a proper family meal with him. But this is an important part of his social development, not to mention his eating skills, and the sooner you start educating him the better. Organising family meals, whenever possible, will emphasise the existence of your family structure (whatever form that may take), reinforce communication and encourage discipline. At the same time, meals should be enjoyable occasions!

It almost goes without saying, that eating together at a table is a vital part of the family meal experience. If your toddler can sit on the same type of chair as you, then all the better. If you have space, you can encourage your child to learn good habits by giving him his own miniature table and chair for everyday meals.

Past the age of one, your child will be able to eat virtually the same food as you, so try to make the menu the same for everyone to help your child feel that he is really part of the family. Keeping the food simple is also a good idea in order to ease stress in the kitchen, especially if you suspect that not all of it will be eaten! If he's able, ask your child to help prepare some of the food or help lay the table. The important point is to be as relaxed as possible, expect mess and disruption, and remember that it's part of a long-term plan to develop a strong and supportive family unit.

Feeding issues

Many toddlers will go through a faddy stage and may absolutely refuse to eat certain foods, while at other times choose the same food day after day. Fortunately, all foods provide some nutrients and no one food is essential to health. Most feeding problems resolve themselves in time, and if your child is growing, gaining weight, and has plenty of energy, then he is unlikely to be nutritionally deficient. No normal child will voluntarily starve himself – when he needs food, he will ask.

Fussy eaters

Toddlers not only routinely refuse certain foods while gorging on others, they often develop a taste for rituals, for example only eating sandwiches that have been cut in triangles, or only drinking out of a yellow cup.

It's incredibly frustrating to spend time preparing a meal that is then not touched, or is simply thrown on the floor. But try to humour

John's story

I'm out of the house for 12 hours a day and don't get home till 7 pm, so there's very little chance of eating with the children. Our four-year-old and two-year-old eat together at 6 pm, at a small table and chairs in the living room. My wife and I eat about 9 or 9.30 pm. We're all up at 6 am so I manage to eat breakfast with the children. At the weekend we have 'special' breakfasts together, usually involving chocolate croissants, and then in the evenings we try to have a family meal at around 6 pm, all eating the same food at the dining table. It's messy, but great fun, and the kids really look forward to it.

your toddler's whims as much as possible. Becoming annoyed will probably only lead to a power struggle that nobody can win. His refusal of food is just one way of asserting his growing independence. And when you think about it, adults are not expected to eat all types of food, so why should this little individual, with an appetite and preferences of his own?

Junk food

Obesity and tooth decay in children are now common concerns among parents. The cause is usually, of course, a diet high in fat and sugar. While there is no need to completely stop giving your child treat foods such as crisps and chocolate, try to limit them to certain days of the week, and avoid sweetened and fizzy drinks.

Messy eaters

For some children, food is an adventure. They do everything with their meal apart from eat it. Again, the way to deal with this is to remember that it's just a phase; try to stay calm and avoid the situation deteriorating into a power struggle. Cover the floor around your toddler with a plastic sheet, buy a bowl that sticks to the table, use a rubber bib with a large food-catching lip, and then just let him get on with it.

WE NEED TO TALK | ABOUT EATING HABITS

You're worried that your child is eating too much junk food during the day, and frustrated because you're at work and have very little influence over his daily diet. Having said that, you're not the person facing the daily battle of getting your son to eat anything at all, let alone the healthy options. Sometimes the only way to manage difficult behaviour is by offering a food treat, and over a long day there doesn't seem anything wrong in that. Your partner is simply taking one meal at a time and trying to make the best of it. But if you really want to address your toddler's eating habits, the first thing for you and your partner to do is take a look at the bigger picture. Ask her to keep a diary of your son's food intake over a week, and then make a judgment about whether there really is a problem, and if so when are the most obvious times when you can start to make changes to his diet.

Allergies and intolerances

Food allergies are actually very rare in children and the symptoms are usually extreme. Intolerances are more common and simply mean that one food does not suit your body as well as others. Don't force your toddler to eat a food that he consistently refuses. It may be that it doesn't agree with him, so try to replace it with a healthy alternative. If you suspect that your child has a food allergy or intolerance – he develops a rash, upset tummy or diarrhoea, then it's wise to consult your doctor.

Activities and play

Play is a vital part of a child's learning and development, and children love copying adults, so it's important that dads are involved as much as possible. Of course, you will not always feel like playing, and it's okay to say so when you really need a break. Children also need to take time out sometimes, or to play quietly alone. But if you can, try to play with your toddler every day, even if it's just for a short time with simple games such as pointing and naming objects, I-spy, or sticker books. Even talking to her, giving her your undivided attention, will be of benefit. At best, let your hair down and have fun – it should help you relax and forget about the pressures of work for a while.

WE NEED TO TALK | ABOUT TELEVISION

Your child's use of the media in general is going to be a recurring issue for you until the day she leaves home, and you and your partner will need to think carefully about the family's policy on watching television. Recent guidelines from US academics advise that children under two years old should not watch any television, while older children should not watch more than two hours a day. The guidance is based on a series of studies that suggest watching television can have adverse affects on a child's mental health, intelligence and behaviour.

Your partner will need time to keep the household under control, as well the occasional break from tending to a demanding toddler, so allowing your child to watch television may be the only answer. But it's important to know how much your child is watching and the quality of the programmes so a good start would be to keep a week's diary of your child's viewing habits. There are also ways to limit the impact. Avoid letting your child watch grown-up television, particularly news programmes with their unpredictable content. Don't leave her alone with the television unless you are totally sure about what she's going to see, and remember that adverts may contain unsuitable topics. Try to avoid watching grown-up television when your toddler is with you – she will be picking up what's going on even if she doesn't seem to be interested. Stick to DVDs wherever possible and dedicated children's channels that you can trust.

The experts say that, ideally, a pre-school child should only watch high-quality educational programmes, accompanied by a parent who talks to her about the content and encourages the same sort of interaction as if they were reading a book together. While this may seem totally unrealistic, especially if you have another older child, at least it gives you an idea of best practice.

WAYS TO PLAY

Different types of play are essential to nurture different skills and prevent boredom.

Reading

It's never too early to start reading books to your child. Every turn of the page brings a surprise, and she can point and learn as you read out loud to her. This is great one-to-one time, so try to do it every day, ideally at the same time, such as bedtime. Put plenty of expression into your voice to really bring the book alive, and point at the pictures as you speak, so your child learns that they are linked to the words. Make relevant noises where appropriate, such as animals or cars, and encourage your child to copy you.

Drawing and painting

Scribbling, drawing and painting are excellent ways for your toddler to express herself, and it's fascinating to keep her artworks in a folder and see how her style and abilities develop over time. You can join in and remind yourself how bad you are at drawing. Colouring books and crayons are

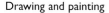

always worth having to hand. Lying on the floor alongside your child, quietly colouring the same picture, can be a real bonding opportunity and a very relaxing pastime.

Messy play

Contrary to popular belief, not all child's play is messy. But most is, and some play is much more messy than others. Top-of-the-range messy play includes splashing around with water, digging in a sandpit, moulding playdough, and, of course, cooking and painting. These are all great fun, giving your child the opportunity to explore a variety of materials and encouraging her to make use of her different senses.

Cooking

The idea of cooking with your toddler sounds like a lot of fun. But before you make the announcement, take a good look at the recipe you are planning to use and work out how long it will take to make, including cooking time. Even something like iced biscuits can take several hours, once you have made the dough, cut the shapes, baked them, waited for them to cool down, mixed up the incredibly sticky icing sugar, and decorated the biscuits. Then you wait for the icing to set, while fighting off a now rabidly hungry child and trying to hose down the kitchen, yourself and your child. Good advice would be to take account of the length of your child's attention span (not to mention your own) and consider making the biscuits without icing – or using some form of quick setting, ready-prepared icing.

Creative play

All toddlers love making things so it's a good idea to have a craft box where you collect usable items such as coloured tissue, toilet rolls and egg boxes. Crafts are an ideal rainy day activity, and the bonus is that at the end of it your child has a new toy to play with – usually a flimsy cardboard tractor, robot or something halfway between the two. It's also fun to make greetings cards for special occasions.

Whatever you decide to do, it's best to start things off yourself and then let your toddler take over. Be very admiring of her efforts and avoid any criticism of the finished product – even if a tractor would never have square wheels.

Imaginative play

This type of play is good to encourage because it doesn't cost anything. All your child needs is a little imagination and it can be fascinating to watch what she invents from a few old clothes and a sheet hung over some chairs in the shape of a tent. On the other hand, children's fancy dress is now big business and no movie is released without a range of mini costumes being available for your child to recreate the story at home – albeit at only slightly less cost than the original budget for the film. This kind of role play is an excellent way for your child to hone all sorts of social and creative skills, even if it does mean you spending weekends as one of the ugly sisters, a troll or the beast.

Music and dance

You'll take a major step towards protecting your sanity if you can persuade your toddler to enjoy grown-up music, especially when it comes to long car journeys. But whatever music she enjoys, make the most of it. Toddlers love to sing and dance so it's a really good way of changing a child's mood, whether you play it yourselves on makeshift instruments, or turn on the stereo for some lively Latin beats. You can prolong your child's interest by introducing games such as musical chairs or statues. Not only is dance great fun, it's also good physical exercise and helps improve a child's co-ordination and balance.

Your toddler's bedtime

By the time your child has hit the toddler stage, you will hopefully have worked through many of the problems usually associated with putting him to bed. Inevitably, the changes in your child that make the toddler years so challenging will still rise up occasionally to destroy your evenings. But once your child reaches the age at which he can understand why he is going to bed, bedtime can become much less of a chore and more of a magical time for you both.

If your partner has so far taken the lead on the nightly routine, now is the time to review the situation so that you can take a more active role. This is quality time with your child, of which you get very little during the week, and it's essential to keep up the bonding process and maintain your relationship as he goes through this exciting period in his development.

Routine is still the vital component of successful bedtimes and both partners have to be committed to getting it right. But what happens in the daytime also has a huge influence on how your child behaves in the evening (see box, below).

Bedtime strategies

Every child is different and each family will need to work out the best times and activities to suit the circumstances, but there are a number of principles to bear in mind to ensure your child goes to bed happily and sleeps through the night.

The hours leading up to bedtime should all be aimed at calming your child after a long day. If he has spent the day in childcare, it is particularly important to bring down his stress levels with lots of attention, cuddles and stroking. It has been shown that if a child does not get this relief in the evening, the stress will still be there when he wakes.

Try to keep his bedroom reasonably tidy and toys out of sight wherever possible – you need to keep your toddler focussed on the task in hand. Dim lighting will calm the atmosphere and help hide the toys, and a nightlight could also counter fears of the dark. Curtains or a blind with a black-out lining will be particularly helpful in the summer when he will ask awkward questions such as 'Why am I going to bed when it's still light outside,' or 'Daddy, why are you still in bed when it's light outside?'

WE NEED TO TALK | ABOUT BEDTIME ROUTINES

A common problem is that the parent caring for the child during the day – let's say it's your partner – is struggling to implement a sleeping pattern that will leave your child tired, but not overtired, at bedtime. If it's a difficult day, your toddler is tired and irritable, and your partner is falling behind on what she needs to do, she may be forced to let him have an extra nap. You then come home to a very lively child, or faithfully go through the whole bedtime routine only to find that your son is not the least bit tired. And the amazing thing about an extra 20-minute daytime nap is that it usually translates into two hours of night-time energy! A similar situation occurs when your child is given chocolate or a sugary dessert close to bedtime, 'to keep him quiet', and it's dad who has to pick up the pieces at bedtime. So both you and your partner have to be committed to a full sleep-management routine before you can properly put it into action.

Stories are the real joy of bedtime, and your child should be looking forward to the experience. Take care when choosing the books that you will read – not too many words, not too scary or exciting – and familiarize yourself with the story beforehand. If your partner is choosing library books during the day, then make sure she knows what to avoid. She might be forced to give in to toddler pressure for a particularly inappropriate book or to just grab a handful in a rush and you then have to struggle through a 'children's' encyclopaedia of Icelandic horror stories!

Essentially, your job is to gently bore your child to sleep. As you will know by now, children are often happy to hear the same story again and again, so don't disappoint. And do everything very slowly – spending a bit more time on the stories will help ensure he goes to sleep soundly, rather than just nodding off and calling you back as you tiptoe down the hall.

After one book, with him sitting up in bed, ask him to lie down ready for sleep and turn out the lights. Now let him fall asleep listening to you telling a story, ideally one that he has requested. Sometimes your toddler will say, 'Make up a story, daddy,' which is probably the last thing you want to hear after an exhausting day at work. One way around this is to tell a classic story but replace the main character with your child. You also could use a song or nursery rhyme as the basis for a simple story. Quietly singing a lullaby can be a good alternative, especially if he seems close to sleep.

If you are sharing bedtime duties with your partner, make sure you both follow the same routine and tell each other afterwards how it went and what stories you told. This is essential to ensure consistency in the bedtime routine and also prevents a mischievous child playing you off against each other.

THE SMITHS' SCHEDULE

This simple routine works well for one couple, who like to keep their three-year-old daughter awake until dad returns from work at about 7 pm, when he takes over the childcare.

5:30 pm   Calming DVD or television.
6:15 pm   Dinner with non-sugary dessert.
7:00 pm   Father returns.
7:15 pm   Relaxing bath for child
7:30 pm   Use potty. Dress for bed. Read book.
7:50 pm   Lights out. Tell story.
8:00 pm   Child falls asleep.
6:30 am   Child wakes up.

Out and about

By the time your child is toddling, you will already have gained lots of experience of going out as a family, and also as a lone father with pushchair and baby attached. But your child's newfound independence means that trips to the outside world become a more taxing proposition, especially if you go without your partner in the hope of some quality, one-to-one time. A lot of couples build this into their weekend schedule, so that dad looks after the child on Saturday morning, for example. As enjoyable and fulfilling as this may be, those four or five hours can seem a very long time for someone who is not used to keeping a toddler entertained.

The first question you ask yourself is: 'Where will we go?'. This decision is crucial to the success of the trip, because the choice of location will have knock-on effects on virtually everything else that you do. So it's a good idea to ask your partner for advice. You may feel that you want to try somewhere different from her regular haunts, but for the first few times you go out alone with your toddler, it's best to play it safe and take advice from the expert. You also could opt for safety in numbers and arrange to meet other dads and their children.

Another good tip is to expect everything to take a lot more time than if you were on your own or with your partner, so build in plenty of extra time to cater for dawdling, tantrums and mishaps.

What to do and how to do it

The arrival of your baby forces you to see your local area from a totally new perspective. Certain restaurants and shops disappear off your radar and they are replaced with new, child-friendly destinations that you didn't know existed before. Suddenly you feel like a tourist discovering the area for the first time. In fact, it's worth contacting your local tourism office for information on child-friendly attractions, and finding out from your local government body what leisure services they provide. If you have a local library, it's likely to have a strong focus on activities for children, and going there to choose books and movies can be an excellent rainy day option.

Eating out in a café or restaurant may seem an attractive idea at first, but is bound to present a whole new range of issues to consider, so

WE NEED TO TALK | ABOUT HOLIDAYS

Before you set off on holiday with your toddler, you need to discuss the ground rules with your partner. A change of routine is usually a great way for adults to wind down, but it's different for small children and the result can be anything but a relaxing holiday! It's very tempting to let all routine drop while you're away, so that your children eat and sleep at different times than they do at home. You want them to enjoy themselves but the problem is that young children need some sort of everyday routine to help them feel secure. They naturally push at the boundaries, and if it means they can stay up all evening they will give it their best shot. As the holiday progresses, they, and you, become increasingly frazzled. So it makes sense to agree a compromise with your partner before you set off, giving the children more freedom but maintaining a routine that you can all work towards. Happy holidays!

it may be best to take packed lunches at first, and leave the more formal meals for family outings when you can share the care with your partner.

Children love picnics so take advantage and make them real occasions, just like the tea parties they organise for their dolls and teddy bears. Your child can help choose the food and pack the hamper. She will be more likely to eat food that she is used to and the whole outing will be much less stressful than a visit to a café or restaurant.

The key elements of a great day out for a toddler are lots of space and opportunities for physical activity, things to see and touch, especially animals, treats such as ice cream, and a souvenir to take home. If you can combine all of these attractions, then you should be heading for a really good time.

You can always liven up a basic excursion to the shops or to the park by putting in a little extra thought beforehand. For example, ask your toddler what to add to a shopping list and then look for the items when you reach the store. Or, the visit to the park can develop into a nature trip by exploring the wildlife, insects and flowers you see there. Follow up your park visit by creating a picture from leaves that you collected, or find books about children doing similar things. And while you are out and about with your child, make the most of opportunities to communicate, for example by pointing out sights and sounds as you walk along together.

When deciding where to go, ask yourself ...

- Do other parents take their children there?
- Is it easily accessible with a pushchair?
- Are the staff and facilities child-friendly?
- Are there likely to be toilet and baby changing facilities?
- Is there a shop nearby for things you might forget or need more of?
- Are the boundaries secure enough to prevent your toddler escaping?
- Are there likely to be crowds, making it easy to lose your toddler?

Potty training

After a year or so of changing nappies you are probably starting to wonder when you can finally hang up your changing mat. You now can do the job with your eyes shut, and the cost of nappies is expensive.

Unfortunately, you have to put up with it for quite some time to come. There is no magic age for potty training but most children will not be dry during the day until they are about three years old. Your child's nervous system has to develop to the point where he can recognise the signs of a full bladder or bowel. He then needs to be able to control his muscles long enough to reach the potty. This combination rarely occurs before two years so there really is no point rushing into a process that is physically impossible for your child to achieve. You'll just face a huge amount of frustration, not to mention anxiety for your child, when you could be spending time on another parenting issue or, indeed, taking a break.

Beginning training

Eighteen months is the earliest age to start training, with around two years the most realistic. There are no hard-and-fast rules, but girls may be more ready from about 18 months, and boys nearer to 30 months.

Whatever age you decide to start training your child, choose a period when you can give him the time and encouragement needed. If you are going on holiday, moving house, or have just had another baby, then leave potty training until things have settled down. Potty training is also easier in warm weather when your child has less clothes to cope with.

Getting started

Begin by explaining in simple language what you want him to do. Teach him what words to use when he needs to pass water or open his

bowels. Let him know that it's a good thing to pooh or wee in a potty.

It may be a good idea to let him pick a potty in his favourite colour. Make sure it has a rigid base to stop it tipping over and that there are no rough edges. For a boy, buy one with a splash guard. Keep the potty in the same place, where he can get to it easily, and where it won't topple over. If you have an upstairs and downstairs, it is a good idea to have potties in different parts of the house. Make sure the area where he uses it is warm.

Dress him in clothes that are easy to take off and teach him how to pull his clothes down. Trainer pants may be useful and are easier to remove than nappies. They also may make your child feel more 'grown up'. Later on, let him go shopping with you to choose his own underpants to wear.

Put him on the potty regularly, such as after meals and before going out, and stay with him

in the early stages. Encourage your toddler to sit for a few minutes – let him look at a book or read him a story. If he sees you sitting on the toilet he may catch on more quickly.

If you have a boy, don't insist that he stands to wee – it is usually easier to sit at first. If he wants to stand, let him use a block to reach the toilet bowl.

When your child uses the potty successfully, give him some praise and encouragement – but not too much. If he doesn't get a result next time, he may become disappointed. Don't expect results too soon and don't nag or force the issue. Expect the occasional accident even after you think your child has become dry and be matter of fact about cleaning him up.

If your child fails to perform, refuses to use the potty, or wets himself, don't get angry. If he becomes anxious about toilet training and there is a battle between you and your child, put the potty away for a week or two or until your child is more ready. Never nag your toddler or force him to sit on the potty.

Using the toilet

As your child gets older, you will need to teach him to use the toilet. (Some children who start training later may insist on using one from the start.) Letting your child copy you using it will get him used to the idea.

It is important that your child feels safe and secure when sitting on the toilet and you may find a special child's lavatory seat useful. Your child will also need a sturdy stepstool or box in order to reach the seat and to rest his feet on. Boys also may need a step to stand up to wee.

Some children are afraid of falling down the hole; if this is the case with your toddler, you will need to hold him on at first.

You should help your child get used to using other people's toilets by letting him use

them when you are out visiting. You should also take him to toilets in public places. Show him how to use the various toilet paper dispensers but carry sufficient tissues in case they are lacking. Make sure your child understands that extra care of hygiene must be taken in public toilets. Teach him to check that the seat is dry and to wipe it down with toilet paper if necessary. Make sure he washes his hands extra thoroughly afterwards.

Going through the night

Learning to stay dry throughout the night usually takes children a little longer than staying dry during the day. Your child has to recognise the feeling of a full bladder while asleep and respond either by 'holding on' until morning or waking up and going to the toilet. About a quarter of three-year-olds wet the bed and need to wear a nappy, so don't be in any hurry to remove the plastic sheet and try not to lose your patience with frequent night accidents.

You can make it easier for your child to stay dry at night by making sure he doesn't have fizzy drinks, citrus juices or drinks with caffeine such as tea, cola and chocolate before going to bed. These can stimulate the kidneys to produce more fluid. Don't reduce the amount your child drinks, however, as the bladder tends to adjust and holds less fluid. It is better that his bladder learns to hold a larger capacity.

You can help your child and minimise your own work by putting a small rubber sheet on top of the child's ordinary sheet with a half sheet over that. If there is an accident, you can quickly remove the half sheet and spare the rest of the undersheet. Most importantly, stay calm and don't make a big deal about it. Bed wetting up to the age of five is normal and while it may be discouraging to change wet beds you should try not to get angry with your toddler. Putting a potty in the room may help and you should make sure he isn't afraid to get up at night, for instance by installing a nightlight.

Possible problems

Fear of flushing is very common and can cause problems with toilet training. Let your child acclimatise to flushing gradually; flush the toilet when he is out of the room but within earshot. When this no longer worries him, try holding him in the doorway while the toilet is flushed. Try doing this nearer and nearer to the toilet until he is ready to pull the lever himself. Your toddler may actually fear flushing away a part of

himself. Waving goodbye to the stool before you flush the toilet may help.

For some children fear of the toilet results in 'holding on', particularly to bowel movements, resulting in constipation. For others it may lead to passing bowel movements in their pants or on the floor. If this is the case with your child, don't insist that he use the toilet, just let him use the potty until he is ready to give it up. Also, give him privacy in the bathroom as he may feel self-conscious, although you should make sure he can't lock himself in. Let him take as long as he needs to go. He could read a book if he wants to – this may help him to relax.

A previously toilet-trained child may regress and start to pass motions in the wrong place; this may be due to physical illness or an emotional upheaval, for example following the arrival of a new sibling or moving house. This will usually resolve itself in its own time. It is important that you stay calm and don't make a fuss about it.

If you discover your child playing with the contents of the potty (a fairly common event), stay calm and do not make him feel ashamed of what he's done but explain that this is not acceptable for many reasons, including hygiene. Tell him that his stool belongs in the potty and must stay there. Divert him from further interest by providing materials for more acceptable creative play, such as finger painting or playing with plasticine. If you find it impossible to divert him, consult your health visitor.

At some stage, your toddler will probably develop an interest in how the opposite sex urinates. Explain the reason for the sitting/standing policy (a boy's stream aims out and a girl's down). If your little girl, for example, persists on trying to stand, let her have a go. After a few tries she will probably discover the disadvantages for herself.

Safety issues

Now that your child is standing and walking, you need to re-think your home safety strategy. The following pages aim to point out the main problem areas and possible ways to minimise the dangers indoors and out.

But there is also a special warning for dads who do too much DIY – yes, it is possible! Addressing safety issues is a great way for fathers to use their practical skills to demonstrate a caring attitude. But this will backfire if, in trying to emphasise your concerns, you become obsessed with DIY, or come to see it as a convenient escape route from some of the less appealing household chores. Believe it or not, there is a limit to how much your partner will appreciate your efforts. There comes a point where she would much rather have you spend a couple of hours on childcare than fitting that third stairgate on the same flight of stairs while listening to the football.

Accidents both outside and inside the home are the most common cause of death and injury among young children, therefore it is vital to protect your toddler from danger. The trick is to do so while not stifling her natural curiosity and growing independence.

Some accidents may happen no matter what your child's age – such as slipping on a rug on a polished floor; others depend on your toddler's level of development – your child would have to be at least two before she'd be able to unscrew bottles and drink the contents. While it is impossible to make your home completely accident proof, or to keep your eyes on your

toddler 24 hours a day, you do need to stay one step ahead of your child by taking appropriate safety measures around your home. A child under the age of three cannot be expected to understand and remember everything you tell her about danger and safety. But as she grows and in line with her level of understanding, you can teach her about dangers and simple accident prevention.

WE NEED TO TALK | ABOUT SAFETY

Your partner wants you to address all the different safety issues in the home, but makes you feel like a criminal every time you get out your toolbox. So important jobs are not being done, or not being done properly, and if your baby has an accident who will get the blame? The first step to resolving this problem is to write a list with your partner of all the safety jobs that need to be done. Then agree the order of priority. When you look at it objectively, perhaps there is too much to do and it would be better to pay a handyman to do everything in a day? Otherwise, a good idea is to agree a time each week, say between 9 am and 10 am on Sundays, when you will start to tackle the jobs, one by one, until the list is finished.

Keeping your child safe

Between the ages of 15 months and two years, your child is likely to be walking confidently, climbing, and be into everything. He will open your drawers and cupboards, be fascinated by water, and grab and pull things such as leads on kettles, teapots on tables, and hanging tablecloths. Your child will have no sense of danger – and will be starting to copy many of your actions. If he sees you smoking a cigarette or drinking alcohol from a glass, for example, and these items are then left lying around, he may be tempted to eat or drink them.

From the age of 15–18 months your child can understand simple instructions and the meaning of the word 'No', if this is said in a firm voice. Be careful, however, not to overuse it: saying 'No' for every minor action your child does may result in him ignoring it when he is really in danger. Your child can also begin to learn the consequences of some actions – such as, if he touches something hot, it will hurt.

By the time your child reaches three he will understand and remember what danger means. You will then be able to start to teach him how to do or use things safely; however, you should never overestimate his understanding. He will lack the experience to estimate danger accurately, even if he seems mature for his age.

It is not always easy to steer a middle path, but overprotecting your child can be as dangerous as underprotection. If your child is not allowed to do anything on his own for fear that he will get hurt, he may become defiant and take unnecessary risks, or become nervous and be more likely to have an accident.

PREVENTABLE DANGERS

A home contains many potential sources of accidents of which you need to be aware. Most accidents are preventable but toddlers, with their boundless curiosity and newfound agility, need a lot of protection.

Choking, strangulation and suffocation

As your child grows older, choking becomes less of a danger but he can still gag on small objects such as food. Until he is five, do not give your child boiled sweets or whole nuts; peanuts are especially dangerous as they can be inhaled, and contain aracis oil which can damage the lungs.

Be careful not to leave small objects around which your child could swallow. Check toys do not have small detachable parts. Take particular care with button batteries as they may contain mercury that can leak if swallowed. If your child swallows one, take him to the nearest emergency department immediately.

Make sure there are no trailing wires or cords which he could wrap around his neck. Don't let appliance cords dangle and use curly flexes wherever possible. Don't let your child wear clothes with drawstrings around the neck.

Keep deflated balloons, polythene bags and plastic away from your child – he may suck these into his mouth and choke or suffocate.

Scalds, burns and chemical injuries

Children's skin is thinner than an adult's, so they can be burnt or scalded at lower temperatures. Don't leave hot drinks or dishes of hot food within reach of your child. When cooking, turn panhandles inwards, and try to use the back burners only. Cooker or hob guards will prevent your child pulling a pan on top of himself.

Liquid tablet forms of household detergent may contain concentrated alkaline. Don't let your child hold them; if he squeezes them hard enough, they could burst and spray alkali into his eyes, causing injury.

Keep your hot water temperature turned down to 54°C, to help prevent scalding. It is not a good idea to leave a hot water bottle in your child's bed.

Keep a fixed fireguard in front of gas, electric or open fires, and in front of open or wood burning stoves. Don't put mobile fires where they can be knocked over, or hang mirrors above fires. Fit smoke detectors on the ceiling of every level of the home. Buy one made to approved safety standards and follow the manufacturer's instructions for fitting. Test it regularly to make sure it is working and replace the battery when necessary or at least once a year. Make sure your child's night-clothes are fire resistant and furniture is covered in fire retardant material.

Keep matches and cigarette lighters out of his reach.

Drowning

A young child can drown in just a few inches of water so never leave your toddler unattended in the bath, even for a few moments. If the telephone or doorbell rings, ignore it or take your child out of the bath before answering.

Don't leave buckets of water around – your child may fall into them and be unable to get out.

Always supervise your child if he's playing near water and fence off garden ponds or cover them until your child is older.

Cuts and gashes

Low-level or fixed glass in and around doors and low cupboards can break if your child bumps into it. It is wise, therefore, to replace this with safety glass or plywood. Or, cover the glass with safety film; this will not stop the glass breaking but it will hold the shards together and can reduce the risk of a serious accident.

If you have a paper shredder at home, keep it stored unplugged and out-of-reach and never allow children to use it, even under direct supervision.

Poisoning

Lock harmful products such as chemicals, medicines and cleaning materials away or put them where your child cannot reach them.

Keep medicines and other potentially harmful products in containers with child-resistant tops, but remember these are not childproof. Don't leave tablets in your handbag or pockets and never refer to them as sweets.

Put poisonous house plants well out of your child's reach and teach him not to eat or pick anything from the garden without asking you first.

Tumbles and falls

Windows should have fitted locks or catches to prevent your child opening them more than 10 cm. However, make sure that you are still able to open them easily in case there is a fire. Windowsills should not be accessible for your child to climb on, nor should they provide a ledge to sit on. If you can, move furniture such as beds or chairs, so that they are not directly under the windows.

Floors should be non-slippery and scatter rugs should be avoided on polished floors.

Try to wipe up any spills immediately.

Furniture should be stable and not tip over easily. Highchairs need to be sturdy with both a waist and a crotch strap. Yours should be secure enough to stop your child standing up in it.

Fit protectors on sharp table corners. Put small objects and ornaments out of reach.

Fit safety gates at the top and bottom of the stairs. Remove only when your child confidently walks up and down without too much danger of him falling. Check that he cannot fall or squeeze through, crawl under, or climb over, banisters or landing rails. If necessary, block these up with hardboard or close netting.

Shocks and electrical burns

Modern electrical sockets are designed not to shock, but if any are easily accessible, fit covers. You should, in any case, teach your child not to put his fingers or any objects into sockets and tape down switches so that he can't turn them on.

Check, too, that you have no frayed electrical cords and that your wiring is not too old, as these can cause a fire.

Avoid buying electrical goods from second-hand shops or markets as you have no guarantee of their safety.

OUTDOOR SAFETY

As well as taking measures in your home, you will also need to make sure your child is safe when he plays outside, or when you visit other people's homes.

SAFETY IN THE SUN

Although children need some sun and fresh air to keep healthy, you need to protect your child from over-exposure to the sun. Not only is sunburn very painful for your child, but every sunburn increases him risk of getting skin cancer in later life. And the fairer he is, the greater the danger.

Keep your child out of the sun when it's at its strongest – this is usually between 11 am and 3 pm. Always protect his skin with a sunscreen formulated for children. Reapply often, especially after swimming. Use a waterproof sunscreen while in the water.

Always encourage your child to play in the shade but watch out for surfaces such as snow, sand, water, concrete and glass, which can reflect the sun's rays. Children also can get burnt on cloudy or overcast days, so always apply sunscreen in the summer even on a dull day.

Don't let your child wear cheap sunglasses in the sun – you need to protect his eyes with sunglasses with an ultra-violet filter.

If your child does get sunburnt, cool him with a tepid bath, shower or cool compress. Apply calamine lotion or an after-sun cream. Don't burst any blisters. Give him cool drinks as he may be dehydrated, and a dose of paracetamol. Keep him indoors.

If your child has severe sunburn, or is shivering, feverish or vomiting, see your doctor.

ROAD SAFETY

When you take your toddler out walking, use reins or hold his hand firmly to keep him securely by your side. If he is in a buggy, fasten his harness every time and take care not to overload it with shopping in case it tips over. Teach him road safety by your example: find a safe place to cross and explain why you have to stop, look and listen, before crossing the road. Teach your child to look out for the 'green man' and the 'red man' at pedestrian traffic lights. Don't let your child go near a road or cross on his own.

IN THE CAR

Make sure you comply with the law regarding the use of child seats, restraints and where he sits in the car. Ensure your child's car seat is correctly fitted according to manufacturer's instructions. If in doubt, have it fitted professionally. Also, fitting child locks on the doors is a must.

Never let your child travel in any car, such as a friend's or a hire car, without a suitable restraint.

Inflatable airbags fitted to the front seats of a car are very dangerous to young children. If they inflate they can suffocate or injure children. If your car has front seat airbags, then always fit your child's car seat to the rear seats.

Never leave your child alone in a car, even for a couple of minutes.

IN THE PLAYGROUND

Your child needs the experience of playing outdoors as part of growing up, but again you will need to be aware of potential hazards, such as unsafe equipment, animal mess and ponds. Whenever possible, let him run around in a fenced off play area.

Check that the ground beneath play equipment is soft, and teach your child not to run in front of swings and roundabouts.

Teach your child not to run up to or touch strange dogs without permission.

IN THE GARDEN

Children love the freedom of exploring in the garden and they may love to help you do your gardening, too. But, as in your home, you will need to take some safety precautions to ensure your child can play without the risk of an accident.

Keep children away when building bonfires or having barbecues; clean up any dog or cat faeces straight away; secure the lids of rubbish bins so that your child can't go rummaging and make sure all ladders are locked away so your toddler can't climb them. If your car is parked near the garden, make sure your child is nowhere near it when it's moving or you are working on it.

9

My new best friend

Two is company

Your older baby is now well and truly a toddler. She's probably launched into her 'terrible twos' with great gusto – they actually start from about 18 months – and may be throwing frequent tantrums. It's a fascinating time for parents as they begin to see the first signs of their child's true character emerging. These toddler years, when your baby is now confidently walking and talking, are when you really start to feel that there are three people in your relationship. You have a new best friend.

Building the relationship
Many dads feel that being out at work all day prevents them developing a proper relationship with their child. But research on the effects of mothers working showed no difference in attachment with their children, compared to mothers who stayed at home to care for them. The key factor was that those working women made sure that when they were at home they gave their children as much positive, focused attention, as possible. And there seems to be no reason why this approach should not work for dads in the same situation.

Virtually everything your child does involves some form of learning, and she is influenced by your behaviour from a very early age. She is incredibly curious and will value your role as a teacher, so it's a good idea to build on this part of your relationship, for example, by taking her on nature trips to learn about plants and animals at first hand. Often you will find yourself on a journey back to your own childhood, rediscovering the interest and enjoyment that's possible from the most simple things in life, which many adults lose sight of through familiarity.

You'll reach a more intimate level of interaction if you can physically get down to her level during play – literally sitting or lying on the floor with her, and relaxing together. Also, mums are much less likely to do 'roughhouse' play than dads, so make the most of this bonding opportunity with good, old-fashioned wrestling, chases and ball games.

At the other end of the play spectrum, colouring in pictures together is a quiet, highly focused activity, which brings you closer both physically and mentally, and can be surprisingly relaxing. That is, until you start fighting over who can use the red crayon, or whether princess so-and-so's hair is brown or yellow. Jigsaw puzzles can be similarly engaging and a useful developmental aid.

Another nice way to build connections with your toddler is to cook for her regularly. Choose recipes together and enlist her help in the kitchen. She'll really take notice of this break in her routine and will remember your efforts. Hopefully, she will eat it all up and look forward to the next cookery session with dad.

Outside the home, keep an eye out for classes to take your child to, such as ballet lessons or soft gymnastics. Weekly events like this will build another unique link between you and your toddler, allow you to meet other parents, and give your partner a break.

Usually it's the mums who take their toddlers along to birthday parties while dad is busy with DIY at home, or sitting outside in the car reading a newspaper, unable to face the small talk. But the more you make the effort and go along to these occasions, the easier it gets. So why not take the plunge? You could go as a family at first, then later take your child on your own. You'll soon build up relationships with other dads – who are all feeling the same way – and their children. You'll see and hear what they are going through, pick up tips on childcare, and, quite simply, make new friends. Children's parties can become an important part of your development as a father, and a great way of letting off steam with people who understand your point of view. Eventually, you may even start looking forward to them.

WHAT DOES YOUR CHILD REALLY THINK OF YOU?

Ask your toddler to do an impression of you. What does she come up with? She'll probably surprise you by doing or saying something that you had no idea was part of your everyday behaviour, or certainly not enough for it to be your defining characteristic! This is a very simple exercise but one that can be very illuminating, not to say humbling or even quite worrying. One dad watched in horror as his daughter stomped around the room with a face like thunder, shouting: 'What the hell is going on here?'. In other words, it's probably not something to try in front of new friends or neighbours.

Showing affection

This is not something that all dads feel comfortable with, having had so much of that 'female' stuff bred out of them over the years. If your child has reached the age of two and you're still having difficulty showing emotions, then you really need to tackle the issue. This is the time to let go of any male inhibitions, and clearly demonstrate to your child that you love her, that you enjoy being with her, that you will listen to her and take her seriously. You have to actually tell your child that you love her, and make it a habit that continues throughout your relationship.

You can show your affection in the most simple of ways, whether it be with an easy smile, lots of cuddles, holding hands, or just doing things together. Think about how much importance we place on the body language of other adults to decide whether they like us, or approve of what we are doing. What signals are you sending to your developing child with your body language?

The physical contact that you make through the daily routines such as washing, bathing or even brushing your child's teeth, provides numerous opportunities to show that you care. It's all about building trust and closeness, much as you would do when bonding with a newborn baby.

By now it will be clear that your child's main goal in life is to get as much fun as possible out of every day, and you'll score lots of points for being a willing accomplice. She will also be developing a sense of humour. You'll first notice this when she offers you a toy or piece of her food and then pulls it away, or jumps into your seat when you get up and will not let you sit down again. This is a bonus because laughter is, of course, a great bonding tool for us all. It gives you another level of communication with your child and an extra injection of fun in to your play.

You can also show affection simply by being with your toddler on occasions that are important to her. Aim to plan your annual leave from work so that you have enough holiday left over from your main family breaks to include birthdays, special day trips and events at nursery.

Try to be with her for all of those important 'first times', such as her first haircut, her first day at nursery, her first ride on a train or her first trip to a library. These occasions make great memories for both of you, especially if you remembered to take a camera. You can then use the pictures to make mini-photo albums and scrapbooks together.

But at the same time you shouldn't think that you have to constantly entertain your child with a big clown smile on your face. You deserve a break occasionally, so don't feel bad about letting her play on her own – which is a skill she needs to learn – while you sit in the same room catching up with your newspaper or a good book.

If another baby comes along ...

You may have gone into a second pregnancy thinking that bringing up a baby would be easier the second time around. That is definitely not the case! You will be more experienced and therefore more relaxed about how you care for your newborn. But it's impossible to predict the character of your new baby and how she will compare to your first – will she be a better sleeper or worse?

Looking after two babies is undoubtedly a lot more stressful, noisy, exhausting and time consuming than taking care of one. At the same time, there is also twice the amount of love and happiness around the house, and even though you swear you'll never have another baby, when she starts growing up you may well begin to miss those early days,

WE NEED TO TALK | ABOUT MAKING MEMORIES

Being away from home all day can be particularly difficult for dads during the toddler years, because your child is developing on so many fronts it feels that you are really missing out. A great way of keeping in touch when you're at work, is to start a scrapbook with your toddler. Talk to your partner about this because it will only work with her support. Begin at the weekend and ask your child to carry on through the week. With your partner's encouragement, whenever your child does something fun or significant that she wants to tell you about, she can record it with a souvenir in her scrapbook. You can catch up with her activities when you're next at home, and go through the book with her when you're together.

and wonder if you might just be able to squeeze in a third.

An important part of preparing for a second baby is to ensure that your first child is comfortable with the idea. This is not going to be easy. How would you feel if your wife announced she was going to take on a second husband, or your boss employed another person to sit next to you and do exactly the same job?

Hopefully you will have been able to plan ahead and tackle as many domestic priorities as possible with your toddler before the latter stages of the pregnancy. Challenges such as potty training and waking at night will be much more difficult to handle when you have a second child to look after. And it's wise to avoid introducing any other big changes into your toddler's life while she is growing used to the baby.

After the birth, give your toddler a present 'from the baby', and keep a few more ready for when friends and family visit with gifts for the new arrival. These will help ensure that your toddler does not feel left out, and you can also ask visitors to give her some extra love and attention when they arrive.

WE NEED TO TALK | ABOUT BREAKING THE NEWS

Once the pregnancy is confirmed, it's a good idea to discuss when you will tell your toddler. Your partner will no doubt be heavily focused on the pregnancy and how she is feeling – not helped by having a demanding toddler around her feet all day. But this is an important issue. Nine months is a long time for your child to wait for a new brother or sister, but it's also not something to leave until the last minute. Talk to other parents about their experiences, and plan how and when you will break the news. Having told your child, you can then build up her levels of interest and acceptance as you approach the birth together as a family.

Your toddler is very likely to revert to babyish behaviour when her new brother or sister arrives on the scene. She feels that she is missing out on your attention, which is hardly surprising given that she has been the total focus of your affection since the day she was born. Suddenly, there is competition and she feels abandoned when her parents are engrossed in caring for the baby.

Dads have an important role to play in balancing the family at this challenging time. Mum will be heavily focused on the newborn, especially while feeding, so you need to give more time to your older child, even though it might hamper your bonding with the baby.

Tony's story

For the first three weeks after the birth, our daughter adored her new brother, but then the novelty wore off when she realised that he was here to stay. During a visit to my parents, I overheard her in whispered negotiations with grandma, asking if the boy could be left with them. Another time she asked me if he could be put out with the rubbish. When I asked why, she replied, 'because he is rubbish'. But things changed again after another couple of months. She fell totally in love with him, and it's been the same ever since.

it's best not to leave your toddler alone with her new sibling until you are happy that this babyish phase has passed. Otherwise, there is not a great deal you can do. Just make sure that you find one-to-one time with your toddler every day, keep telling her how special she is and how much you love her, but explain that the baby needs more of your help until she can better look after herself. Ask your toddler to help you look after the baby so that she feels like she is playing a grown-up part in family life. And remind her how clever she is to be able to do so many things that the baby cannot do, and that later she'll be able to teach the baby how to open a door or kick a football. Eventually your toddler will realise that she actually has a great new playmate available 24 hours a day, who copies every move she makes and generally adores her.

Some toddlers will begin talking in a baby voice, others will start wetting themselves again or demanding cuddles in the middle of the night, especially if the baby is sleeping in your room or bed.

Your toddler even may be violent towards the baby. If this happens, make it clear that she was wrong but try not to overreact. Generally,

Girls and boys
Some dads may feel disappointed that their baby is not a boy. But are there any real differences or do we just treat them differently, eventually producing different characteristics? For example, researchers have observed that parents are less likely to help a boy who is crying or in pain, than a girl doing the same. Maybe this is because parents are more protective of the girl but think the boy should 'get on with it'. At a simplistic level, one could imagine that boys

Matt's story

My daughter went through a really awkward phase of refusing to wear anything but dresses. She would scream and fight if we went anywhere near her with a pair of trousers, or even a skirt - and this was in the middle of winter. Eventually we gave up fighting with her and tracked down some thick, woolly dresses and tights. But her reaction had started to rub off on her younger brother, who also started to get stroppy about his clothes. He refused to wear a jumper decorated with a rhino pattern and in the end we had to give it away. Strangely, the boy we gave it to also refused to wear it.

learn to hide their emotions and put up with pain, while girls grow up more likely to show emotion and express their feelings.

Boys are said to be slower than girls at learning to talk, and usually take more of a liking to practical, mechanical games, toys and vehicles, as well as physical play. Girls seem more interested in conversational, interactive play, either with their dolls or acting out roles themselves – usually dressed as princesses.

Girls are also said to be 'better bullies' than boys, because they use intelligent psychological weapons against their victims rather than the brute physical force usually associated with male bullying. Most men will have learnt this fact of life long before they become fathers!

So it's difficult to pinpoint which traits come from nature and which from nurture. But what is clear is that we as parents have a huge influence on the way our children develop and that whatever their genders, we need to respect them as individuals, and treat them accordingly.

Maximising family time

However you felt about your job before the birth of your child, you will definitely be re-evaluating your feelings now. Whatever way you look at it, work takes away time that could be spent with your family.

Things are generally becoming easier for parents in the workplace, as society begins to recognise the importance of parenthood and the raising of future generations. There is also a growing acceptance that achieving a balance between work and home life is a good thing for both employees and their employers.

So the first step towards maximising family time is to check out your company's policies and compare them to national legislation on working hours, because the situation may be more family-friendly than you expected.

Hopefully your immediate boss will have a family of his/her own and appreciate the pressures that you're facing. If not, you need to make sure that your superior, and other close colleagues, know enough about your home life to encourage a sympathetic attitude. But whatever you do, don't become the office baby bore, unable to talk about anything but your wonderful children.

Is there a possibility of flexible working? This would mean being able to cope with minor emergencies at home without having to take annual leave or lose pay, not to mention the goodwill of your colleagues.

You could also use that time to take your child to nursery. This is a good way of meeting other local dads, developing an informal support

WE NEED TO TALK ABOUT DOING YOUR JOB

Your partner will be keeping a close eye on the amount of time you spend at work, because the days at home with a baby can seem very long. Meanwhile, you are also feeling under pressure at work from colleagues who expect you to keep the same office hours as them. Deep down, your partner knows that it's important for the whole family that you keep your job, but at the same time she needs to feel that your heart is in the right place. You need to do everything you can to get home at a good time, sticking as closely as possible to your official working day. So while you're at work, aim for maximum, visible impact during office hours, so that you can avoid starting early or staying late. Use time travelling to catch up or do something extra, and try to make it something that will be noticed. Whether you are using a computer on a train or thinking while walking or driving, this can be a great time for coming up with new ideas or resolving tricky issues.

network, and putting faces to the names of the friends that your daughter is always talking about. Suddenly you are opening up a whole new level of conversation and interaction with your daughter. Make sure you dress her and give her breakfast so that you really take an active part in her daily routine. And, of course, it gives your partner a break from the nursery run, and perhaps even an extra hour in bed.

Finally, it's a sad fact that many dads do not take their full entitlement of annual leave. In the US, the average worker receives less than four weeks of paid leave each year, including public holidays, compared to well over six weeks in the UK. Even then, the average American worker still fails to take four days of his annual entitlement.

Once you feel that you've really maximised the amount of family time in your weekly schedule, the next step is to make the most of it. But that's really up to you and the amount of effort you want to put in. Just don't forget to build in time at weekends for you to spend alone with your toddler, reinforcing the bond and leaving your partner space to recuperate.

Mike's story

I was out working every day and getting home just at the time when my daughter was due to go to bed. I had thought that this arrangement was fine, but gradually began to realise that I had to get home earlier. By bedtime she was usually exhausted and tearful, as was my wife. Other dads have since told me how their household disintegrates into chaos towards early evening, when the stresses of the day finally catch up with everyone. I discussed it with my wife and plucked up the courage to talk to my boss. I managed to move my working hours around, just enough to get home half an hour earlier. It's amazing what a difference such a small amount of time can make. Now they don't reach the crying stage and I get some extra quality time with my family.

10

Changing behaviour

Being a role model

Have you ever thought of yourself as a role model for someone else? Do you have a younger brother or sister who has always looked up to you, or do you manage staff, who would like to follow in your footsteps at work? Has it dawned upon you yet that you are probably going to be the most important role model in your child's life? It's a daunting prospect and consequently most fathers, indeed parents, will avoid the issue and not really analyze how their behavior will influence that of their child – until it's too late to do anything about it.

And this is not just something that's important for your family but for society as a whole. If all fathers were excellent role models, how much would that change society for the good in 20 years' time? But if all fathers were terrible role models, would you want to live in the society that resulted?

Even in the early days of your child's life you will notice him mimicking your behavior,
whether it's stirring a spoon around an empty bowl or copying your sneezes. He is learning from you in the most basic of ways – but copying is the way that we learn everything. Your child will continue copying and learning from you throughout his childhood and adolescence, which puts a heavy weight on your shoulders. And the job of being a role model will be made even more difficult if you start off on the wrong foot and then have to spend time trying to correct the impressions that you gave, once your son is already entrenched in his behaviour.

Developing guidelines

The first place most men will look when seeking guidance in this area is to their own fathers – how did they do as role models? But often there will have been so many different influences in your life, or the qualities are so ingrained in your character, that it may be

We all like to get stuck into our own things but ignoring your child when he wants to talk with you is teaching him that he isn't very important to you.

difficult to pick out exactly what you took from your dad – for better or worse. A good start is to ask your partner. Even if he has not told you before, he will have an insight into the similarities between you and your family, and the traits you have picked up from your father, whether you like what she has to say or not! Either way, this issue is going to take up considerable thinking time, something of which you probably don't have a lot right now. But it is essential to have some sort of guiding principles to hold onto as you go through the fatherhood experience. Not a plan that is rigid and intimidating, but guidelines that will develop as you progress, to provide some solid grounding and structure in your children's lives, that they can work from and grow their own characters.

One way of starting to think about this is to write down the key qualities that you would like to see in your children as adults. Then write a list of your own qualities. How do they compare? At this stage you may want to risk ridicule by showing the lists to your partner and asking whether she agrees. (Maybe she should write her own lists?) If your lists are a reasonable match, then you are already on the right track. But now take the list of your qualities and write down how you demonstrate each of those qualities to your child in daily life. This is the difficult part.

Most of us assume that we are good people and our children will turn out the same. But maybe we should look at our behavior a bit more closely. Children cannot tell the difference between right and wrong, and cannot understand irony. Adults can see through their less attractive habits, and take themselves as a whole package, balancing the good and the bad, knowing that we mean well, even if we do not

always show it. Children, on the other hand, will see us doing things, assume they are good, and adopt them. For example, recent research on bullying in schools suggests that the bullies are used to being frightened and bullied at home by their parents, and naturally replicate that behavior when they are interacting with other children.

So when it comes to influencing your children, it's no good just having a list of guiding principles, you have to live up to those standards and let your children see you doing it. If this all seems too theoretical at the moment, then one area where you can achieve quick, practical benefits for you and your child, is by looking at the way that you and your partner interact as a couple. Your child is going to be heavily influenced in the way he conducts relationships by the way that his parents behave, so aim to keep any difficult stuff private but let your child see, and take part in, the caring, affectionate and communicative relationship that you and your partner share.

Matters of discipline

The way that you guide and discipline your toddler will inevitably affect the way that he grows up and behaves as an older child and adult. Too much authoritarian discipline can leave him unable to make decisions for himself in later life. On the other hand, too little discipline at an early age can mean that he fails to develop any real self control or willingness to accept responsibility for his actions. So it makes sense to follow a more flexible route, which falls somewhere between those two extremes. This approach embraces firm rules, but the discipline is accompanied by explanation, discussion and a degree of independence for your child. He will grow up in a supportive environment in which his needs are respected. Hopefully, this path will lead to a self-reliant, self-controlled and socially aware older child, and eventually an adult of similar qualities.

THE GOLDEN RULES

Be consistent in your approach It's very important that you set reasonable limits and stick to them. Your child will become confused and frustrated if he is allowed to do something one day but is reprimanded for doing the same thing on the following day. Both parents must agree a strategy on discipline and avoid giving your child the chance to manipulate one parent against the other.

Give your child clear guidelines Be specific about the rules rather than making vague statements. Explain why he is being disciplined, for example because he hit someone again after you had told him to stop. And don't punish him twice – if he has already been told off by one parent he should not be disciplined again for the same misdemeanour.

Use language consistently There are many ways of saying the same thing but your child will probably assume they all have different meanings and become confused. For example, all of these words

DIFFERENT TYPES OF PUNISHMENT

Reprimand Children are keen to please their parents, so a stern telling off when they are doing, or have done, something naughty, can be very effective. But it will only work if used sparingly and with conviction. Constantly telling off your child for the slightest misdemeanour will have a negative effect and he will simply stop listening. When reprimanding your child:

- Make sure you have his full attention. Look him in the face by bending down to his level or sitting him up on a chair.
- Your voice should be firm and confident. Keep your words short and to the point, making it clear why you are unhappy.

- Point out the consequences of continued bad behaviour.
- Check that he has understood what you have said.

Time out This is a simple, unemotional and effective way of correcting poor behaviour, or removing your child from a deteriorating situation. When he misbehaves, remove him to a separate room and tell him to sit quietly on a chair that he can climb onto himself. Tell him why he is having 'time out' and leave him there, for about a minute for each year of his age. Ideally, the room should be quiet and unstimulating, such as a hallway. If he leaves the room before the time is up, calmly take him back to the and phrases essentially mean 'No': wait, stay, don't, don't move, don't do that, come back, leave it alone, stop. Try to agree with your partner the simple commands that you want to use and then do so consistently to achieve the right response from your toddler. But remember that over-use of any one command will eventually lead to indifference.

Praise your child When he behaves well, make sure you give your child credit, rather than only commenting on negative behaviour. Positive reinforcement of good habits is the best way to improve his behaviour over the long term.

Don't make empty threats Only threaten punishments that you know you will carry out. For example, saying that he will never be allowed to eat chocolate again is a threat that has zero chance of being implemented. Your toddler will soon realise that you do not mean what you say and discipline at any level will become difficult to enforce.

Give your child a chance Make sure he has the opportunity to try alternative behaviour before you punish him, or give him time to respond to your request. If he's kicking a chair, for example, suggest that he goes outside and kicks a ball. Tell him you will count to ten, and warn him of the consequences if he fails to respond.

Make up with your child afterwards Once you have disciplined your child, let him know that you still love him as much as ever, and then move on to other things.

chair. Repeat as necessary until the time is served, avoiding any discussion. Once the time is up, give him a cuddle and forget the incident. As with all disciplinary techniques, over-use will limit the effect.

Smacking Most parents are tempted to spank their child at some point, and some believe that a short smack is an effective way of dealing with bad behaviour. It should only ever be used as a last resort, if at all. Smacking is forbidden in some countries, and even if it's not illegal, there are very strong reasons why it should be avoided. Firstly, you could injure your child, or lose control of yourself. Secondly, smacking is usually ineffective because the child becomes used to

it. And thirdly, it can induce aggressive behaviour in your child, because he thinks that it must be acceptable if you are doing it to him.

If you do smack your child, it should be done immediately and sparingly – a sharp tap on the hand when he is heading towards danger – and when all other tactics have failed. Only your hands should be used and only one smack given.

Tackling bad behaviour

Children need boundaries to help them regulate their behaviour. Knowing what's expected of them and how far they can go will make them feel safe and secure. Guidelines need to be set and bad behaviour controlled. But a toddler is only just starting to learn how to control his body and behaviour, so any discipline from you must be appropriate to your child's age and understanding.

Even when your child is old enough to understand the rules, it is only normal if he tries to push the limits, just to see what he can get away with. But often you can head off potential conflict by anticipating bad behaviour and removing your child from the scene, being aware of trigger factors, ignoring minor offences and trying to avoid saying 'No' repeatedly.

It can be very easy for modern dads to slip into habits more usually associated with the traditional, disciplinarian father figure. We are probably more inclined to take a tougher line than our partners, due to our own male upbringings. This is reinforced by the natural instinct to help our partner by taking control of the situation, and at first it seems to work. Your toddler may be ignoring your partner's complaints but a stern reprimand from you surprises him and he responds as you wish. However, the impact soon wears off and each night you are left shouting ever louder to get your way. Where will it end?

Discipline within the family is about teamwork – and hard work. You cannot hope to resolve your son's disciplinary problems with a quick fix each evening. If your partner is caring for him through the day, then she is the major influence on his behaviour. But it's not her fault that she's run out of options because, as you know, looking after a toddler is a tough job.

The key to solving the problem is to agree a concerted approach that works for you both, even though it will require a lot of self-discipline from yourselves, and will inevitably take longer to implement than the miracle cure that you (and all other parents!) are looking for.

Try to discuss it at the weekend when there is less pressure, and make gradual changes during the day and night to eventually bring about the desired effect. It has to be a joint approach, applying consistent boundaries with agreed strategies, 24 hours a day. Even then, your toddler will still find gaps, and the end of the day is always going to be stressful, but at least you're on the right track. And at the times when you wonder whether it's worth all the effort, just remind yourself why you're doing it: because you want your son to respect you, not live in fear of you.

WE NEED TO TALK | ABOUT DISCIPLINARY MATTERS

Why are you always left feeling like the bad guy? You get home from work and the house is in chaos. Your son is running riot and your partner's in tears. You complain that she needs to enforce more discipline, and then shout at your son when you can't get him to sleep. Your partner then shouts at you for shouting at your son. By the time the weekend comes, she's had enough of his tantrums so leaves the discipline to you. But then you feel that the little time you have with your son is spent arguing with him. Does that sound familiar? The first thing you need to do is sit down quietly with your partner and try to take a detached overview of the situation. The only way to start tackling the problem is through teamwork. Work out a simple strategy, with a start date. Stick to it, and only change the plan in agreement with your partner.

Tackling tantrums

Most children between the ages of 18 months and three years exhibit uncontrollable rages or temper tantrums occasionally – but some have them more frequently than others. Strong-willed or determined children, for example, have more of them than the placid and easy-going types. With some children a tantrum may be a short outburst of rage that soon blows over but for others it may last for some time, with the child lying on the ground thrashing his arms, kicking and screaming, throwing things or holding his breath.

Having an occasional temper tantrum may actually be good for your child's emotional development. It can release his pent up frustration, and teach him that feeling anger is normal, but that its expression needs to be controlled. It also means that your child has energy and assertiveness that will stand him in good stead later on. But too many tantrums are exhausting for the whole family and can develop into antisocial behaviour. So if your child has tantrums frequently, try to work out the reasons why and, as far as possible, avoid these trigger situations (see causes, below).

Holding breath

It is not unusual for a toddler to hold his breath when in a temper. The child becomes redder and redder and then turns blue or may turn white. The breathing usually starts again at this stage, but sometimes the child goes stiff or floppy or may even pass out. Seeing your child holding his breath is very frightening, but highly unlikely to harm him. If he becomes unconscious after breath-holding, check with your doctor to exclude any medical cause.

WE NEED TO TALK | ABOUT SPANKING

If you manage to avoid spanking your child during the toddler years then you are doing very well. You will certainly come close at times, and it's an issue that you need to discuss with your partner before your child reaches the age where it's a possibility. You need to know how each other feels about the issue, and discuss ways that you can avoid reaching breaking point. If it happens, you will undoubtedly feel guilty afterwards and should talk through the incident, without attaching blame, to hopefully learn from it. Also make sure that if one of you does spank your child, you apologise to him, give him a cuddle and tell him how much you love him.

Otherwise, difficult though it is, ignore your child when he holds his breath – don't slap him or pour cold water on him. In the unlikely event that he becomes briefly unconscious, watch him carefully, but move away as soon as he starts to come round.

Head banging

Between the ages of one and two, if a child does not have his own way or gets into a temper tantrum, he may bang his head against the wall or floor. Although you will worry that your child will hurt himself, injury is rare. If he is otherwise normal, head banging is nothing to worry about and best ignored. Some children also head bang before going to sleep, or if they are tired or bored.

Causes of temper tantrums

- *Attention seeking behaviour* Toddlers love to be the centre of attention, and throwing a tantrum may be one way of achieving this.
- *Frustration* This may result if your child is not allowed to do something he wants to do, he is unable to do something due to limited capabilities, or if he is made to do something he does not want to do. Pick your battles, and don't fight over small things

that do not really matter, such as objecting to him wearing odd socks or not letting him pick what t-shirt to wear.

- *Imitation* He may see and copy another child or adult having a tantrum.
- *Blackmail* He may use a tantrum as a device to get his own way.
- *Tiredness* Tantrums are more common if a child is tired or overexcited.
- *Hunger* Children need to eat regularly, and if mealtimes are too far apart your child may get hungry. Make sure he has some nourishing snacks in-between meals.
- *Inconsistency* Allowing him to do some things, but not others, without any clear guidelines, or one parent saying 'Yes', and the other 'No', is confusing and frustrating for your toddler.
- *Unrealistic expectations* Don't expect too much from your toddler; build in rest time during the day. If too many activities are packed into a day, or you expect him to come shopping when he's been busy at playschool, then an explosion is more likely.

Dealing with tantrums

As far as possible, try to identify trigger situations and avoid them. But if your child does throw a tantrum, try to keep calm and remember that, in time, he will get over this difficult phase.

As he grows older you will be able to talk more about angry feelings, and ways of coping with them. Meanwhile, don't lose your own temper or give in, and don't try to deal with the tantrum using bribes, smacking or threats. Try the following instead:

- *Distract* Point out of the window at something or suggest going to the park.
- *Ignore* If your child does not have an audience, he cannot perform. Put him in a different room until the tantrum is over or, if he is safe, you leave the room. If out in public, decide whether to stay put until the tantrum blows over and ignore any disapproving comments or looks, or whether to physically remove him from the scene with the least possible fuss. If your child is kicking and screaming, move any potentially dangerous objects out of his reach, so that he cannot hurt himself.
- *'Angry toys'* Provide your child with alternative outlets for anger and frustration. Toy drums or other musical instruments may help him work out his feelings and channel them in constructive ways, as will physical activities such as riding a tricycle. You also can encourage him to express

WE NEED TO TALK | ABOUT STRESS BUSTING

Your partner is becoming increasingly stressed by your toddler's difficult behaviour – regular tantrums and constant whining in between. This is actually normal behaviour as your child struggles to come to terms with the world and battles with his own limitations. But that doesn't make it any easier to deal with. The build-up of stress through the day means that your partner is more likely to react badly, and in turn the child becomes more tearful and demanding. It's a vicious circle but you can help your partner lessen the effects. For a start, encourage her to have a complete break from home life by going away for a night or weekend with a friend. Hopefully she will come back feeling refreshed, and more able to take an objective view of the situation. Help her to identify the most problematic periods in the day when she really needs to take a 'time out'. Anything she can do to break the build-up of stress levels will help avoid her feeling overwhelmed towards the end of the day.

himself through colouring, drawing or painting pictures.

- *Join in* If your child is shouting, accompany him for a while, then gradually lower your voice – your child will probably copy you until you are both whispering. This will help show your child that anger is more acceptable when expressed in words, than in physical violence.
- *Make up* Once the tantrum is over, let your child know that it is natural to feel angry and that you feel angry too sometimes. Make sure he knows that you still love him and that it's only his behaviour you don't like. Remember to congratulate him once he has regained control.

Helping your child get on with others

Social skills and behaviour are important for your toddler's eventual emergence as an independent individual. These skills include the ability to meet, mix and communicate with other people; learning how to play, share, take turns with others and accept rules; mastering toilet training and adhering to general standards of cleanliness and eating in 'acceptable' ways. As your child acquires these social skills he will also gain independence and confidence and learn to value himself and others.

Learning how to make friends and get on with people is an essential part of growing up. A child who is friendly and well liked is more self confident, and has more fun and play opportunities.

Not every child is naturally confident and outgoing, however, and, like everything else, the ability to make friends and socialise has to be learnt. Young toddlers are 'egocentric', that is, the centre of their own worlds. Your toddler will be unable to understand the concept of sharing or the feelings of others, and playing with other children often leads to tears over a coveted toy.

As his self-knowledge grows, however, your child should begin to demonstrate that he is aware that what he feels is felt by others; this is known as empathy. He may even respond to another person's distress by becoming distressed himself. Empathy may encourage a child to become more generous and unselfish in play with others and is something you should try to help him to develop.

While aspects of your child's personality may have been apparent at birth (whether he cried a lot or was placid, for example) between the ages of two to three his true personality will become quite obvious.

While he is learning to master the various locomotive and manipulative skills, he will become aware of his ability to influence the actions of himself and others.

When he is unsuccessful in his attempts, he also will suffer from feelings of shame and failure. He must learn to handle both his successes and his failures in acceptable ways in order to become a well-balanced individual.

You can help your child to better integrate the different aspects of personality – activity, sociability and emotionality – by showing him how to tackle problems successfully, distracting him when he becomes frustrated, and by enabling him to construct a positive self-image through praise without ridiculing his fears.

Promoting social skills
- Make sure your child is familiar with other children by going to places where there are other children present.
- Encourage loving behaviour towards other people, animals and dolls.
- Use public transport for outings and visit supermarkets and cafés where he will learn to queue and wait for his turn.
- If there is a dispute with another child over a toy, try not to intervene immediately, but stand by to sort out any fights and introduce the idea of sharing and taking turns.
- As soon as your child becomes old enough to understand, praise any attempts at sharing. At first he may share just to please you, rather than out of any sense of fairness. Suggest that each child take turns to play with a favourite toy. You could set an alarm clock to ring every five minutes or so.
- Teach him to say 'Please' and 'Thank you' at the appropriate times.

Right and wrong
By the age of three you need to make sure that your toddler is aware of the difference between 'good' and 'bad' actions. Try and explain to your toddler in simple ways why you want him to do one thing and not another. Most children like to do what is right, although it doesn't always stop them being naughty, because naughtiness is a very good way of making you pay attention to them.

Rather than concentrating on the negative aspects of personality, the best tack is to use positive reinforcement as much as possible. Give praise when your toddler is careful in situations or with other people's feelings.

Many toddlers mix make-believe and reality or tell you things that are not strictly true. This is not lying but a natural part of behaviour at this age – some psychologists believe that children are only capable of lying after the age of four.

Some children constantly use the word 'No' even when they mean 'Yes' but this is simply their way of trying to assert authority.

Problems with sociability
Some children have trouble focusing their attention on anything for any length of time, including playing with other children. Others go through a phase of temper tantrums, aggressiveness, extreme insecurity or rapid and frequent mood changes. Often this is a natural stage of development and you need not worry. However, if your child's 'bad' behaviour is prolonged or you are having trouble coping with it, ask your doctor or health visitor for some advice.

Baby health guide

Looking after your baby's health

Every year in the UK, women visit their doctors for health advice twice as often as men. It's the same old story about men not feeling the need to discuss their health issues, mental or physical, with anyone else. So it can be a shock for a new father when you have to take your child to the doctor's surgery. You probably won't be familiar with the procedures and etiquette of the waiting room or the consultation, and you may feel uncomfortable having to interpret your child's symptoms for the doctor.

With more dads taking an active role in the care of their children, and research showing how important their involvement is to child health and development, even the medical establishment is now recognising that fathers need more help from doctors. The American Academy of Pediatricians recently published guidance for its members, which went so far as to encourage them to change their practices and clinical style to better accommodate and involve fathers.

A good way to get to know the routine at your local surgery is to accompany your partner when your baby is called in for immunisations. Keeping up to date with all the regular vaccinations is vital for your child's health, but the injections can be a stressful experience for both baby and parents, so it makes sense to support your partner on the first visit, at least.

In the early years of parenting, it can feel like your child is constantly ill as she goes through the necessary chore of contracting almost every illness available in the local community while building up her immune system. This is exhausting for the whole family, especially when the bugs spread. And it's important to be aware of the extra strain your partner is under when she's tending for a sick, demanding child. It can be harder if your partner is breastfeeding, because she may literally be drained of energy by the baby's attempts to gain comfort through continual suckling. While breastfed babies contract fewer infections than bottlefed babies, it won't seem like that at the time.

So, although it's your baby who is ill, it can be a very stressful time for mums and dads, making even minor illnesses much more difficult to handle. When you're up in the middle of the night trying to take a temperature or struggling to administer medicine to a hot, crying baby,

---

WE NEED TO TALK | ABOUT SICKNESS DAYS

When your partner and child are ill at the same time, and your partner is struggling to look after your child, this is when she really needs to feel your commitment to the family. But what if you are under pressure to perform at work and feel torn between the financial and emotional priorities? Your overriding loyalty must be to your family, but you have to be totally honest with your partner. Find out exactly what she feels is possible, or what favours you can call in from friends – you can be sure they will need help in return some day. The longer your partner struggles on, the longer the illness is likely to last. One day of rest may mean she will be better able to cope the following day. Everyone gets ill at some time and taking sick leave to care for your family should be no different than taking it when you are ill. As long as you can maintain your credibility at work, there should be no reason to feel guilty.

A VISIT TO THE DOCTOR

These tips should help you make the most of a visit to the surgery with your sick child, easing anxieties and giving your doctor the best chance of making an accurate diagnosis.

1   Write a list of your child's symptoms and when they occurred.
2   Write down any medicines you have given your child, including the time and dose.
3   Dress your child in clothing that is loose and easy to remove so that the doctor can examine her quickly and easily. Keep your child warm with a blanket or coat, if necessary.
4   If you have not been to the surgery recently, ask your partner what to do on arrival.
5   Take a drink for the baby and nappy changing gear, just as you would on any other trip.

it can be a real trauma trying to decide whether the problem is serious enough to call out a doctor. And research has shown that when a child is feverish, parents tend to take inaccurate temperature readings and then give a child the wrong doses and types of medicine. The key to getting things right in these situations is to have all the necessary equipment and medicines on hand, and to keep a notepad to write down what you do, and what symptoms your child is showing, at what times. This helps you keep control of the situation, and provides a record to help the doctor with diagnosis, should that be necessary. There are also some simple guidelines to follow, which can help take the heat out of the situation (see box).

When to see the doctor

New babies can become ill very quickly, so it is important to be aware of the symptoms that could indicate illness. If your baby develops any of the following symptoms, or appears unwell, urgent medical advice is required.

- Paleness or a bluish colour around the mouth and on the face.
- Fever with a temperature of 38°C (100.4°F) or more.
- Baby's body becomes floppy or stiff.
- Eyes are pink, bloodshot, have a sticky white discharge, or eyelashes that stick together.
- White patches in the mouth.
- Redness or tenderness around the navel area.
- Nose blocked by mucus, making it difficult for your baby to breathe while feeding.
- Diarrhoea – more than six to eight watery stools per day.
- Projectile vomiting.
- Vomiting that lasts for six hours or more, or is accompanied by fever and/or diarrhoea.
- Refusing to be fed.
- Crying for unusually long periods.
- Blood-streaked stools.

When your baby is ill

There are some basic skills you need to master so that you can comfort your sick baby and ensure that medicines are taken effectively. Small children can be very resistant to accepting what's good for them, and it can often require both parents working in tandem to get the medicine down. Don't expect to get it right first time and always have a cloth or tissues available to mop up the spills!

Taking a temperature A young baby's temperature should be taken under her arm. If you're using a digital thermometer, wipe under your baby's arm to remove any sweat, then place the bulb into the fold of her armpit and hold her arm against her side to keep it in place. Leave for three to four minutes or until the thermometer beeps. Contact your doctor if the temperature is raised to 38°C (100.4°F) or more. Always mention that it is an axillary temperature (one taken under the arm), as this has a slightly lower reading.

With an older child, a digital ear thermometer is worth the extra investment, because it takes an instant reading and remembers it. Strip thermometers that can be held against the baby's forehead seem easier but these are often unreliable and difficult to read.

Giving medicine by oral syringe This can be a great alternative to the standard spoon method if your baby is refusing to open her mouth or proving difficult to keep still. Cradle her in your arms and aim the tip of the syringe between her rear gums and cheek, avoiding the taste buds. Squirt the medicine slowly to avoid making her choke, and do not touch the back of the tongue with the syringe in case it causes her to gag.

Giving medicine by dummy-style syringe The nipple-shaped tip on this syringe allows your baby to suck while you express the medicine. Hold your baby in your lap, supporting her head in the crook of your arm. Put the tip of the syringe in her mouth, as you would with a bottle, and slowly press the plunger.

Administering eye drops This can be a tricky operation and it may be wise to swaddle your baby to prevent her wriggling. Lay her on her back and tilt her head to one side, with the affected eye nearest your leg. Taking care not to touch the eye with the dropper, pull down her lower eyelid and squeeze the drops into the eye. You may need help to hold her head steady.

Administering ear drops Lay your baby on her side with the affected ear facing upwards. The medicine needs to be dropped down into the ear canal, so straighten the canal by gently pulling back the earlobe. Bring the dropper close to her ear to ensure you hit the target, and hold her steady while the drops sink in, using cotton wool to soak up any leaks.

Sponging your baby Bringing down your baby's high temperature will comfort her and help her feel less irritable. Wrap her in a towel and sit her on your lap. Gently wipe her down with a sponge soaked in water that has been boiled and then cooled to a lukewarm temperature.

Caring for some common conditions

Colds

Colds are caused by different viruses and your child is likely to have about eight colds a year until age 12, after which immunity builds up. A cough may develop with a cold but if your child is eating and breathing normally and there is no wheezing, usually it is nothing to worry about. Although colds and coughs can cause discomfort they rarely need treatment; antibiotics are not usually prescribed unless a chest infection develops.

Apply petroleum jelly around your child's nose to stop it becoming sore. Keep your child cool and give him plenty of fluids. Avoid overusing cough mixture – a warm drink of lemon and honey can be just as soothing.

Consult your doctor if your child seems to be having breathing difficulties or is wheezing, has a high temperature or seems to be in pain when coughing, or the cough continues for a long time.

Croup

A respiratory infection of the larynx or voice box, croup is caused by a virus or by bacteria. It is common in children up to the age of four. It is characterised by a harsh or barking cough, a runny nose, hoarseness, noisy breathing and fever. Most cases of croup are mild and do not last long. but it can be very alarming.

If your child gets croup, stay calm or you may frighten him more. Reassure him and sit him up. Give plenty of warm drinks and the recommended dose of paracetamol for any fever. A steamy atmosphere may help breathing. This can be relieved by boiling a kettle, running the hot taps in the bathroom, using a humidifier or putting wet towels over the radiator. If using steam, take care to avoid scalding. Keep the door and windows closed and encourage your child to inhale.

However, call your doctor immediately or take your child to hospital if he becomes distressed, or has difficulty in breathing or swallowing, turns blue, or there is indrawing of the ribs or below the ribs, when breathing.

Fever

If your baby has skin that is warm to the touch, is reluctant to feed, is lethargic or shows signs of a possible infection, such as a cold, check whether your baby has a fever. If he is under three months, most doctors would consider a temperature of more than 38°C (100.4°F) to be a fever.

There are several reasons why a baby may develop a fever right after birth. His mother may have an infection that has been passed on to him, for example. Even if the mother has a normal temperature, an infection can cause a fever in her baby. Less likely, a raised temperature can be related to the baby's environment: if the delivery room or nursery is too hot, a baby's temperature may increase.

No matter what the cause, an elevated temperature in a baby should never be ignored; it may be the first indication of a more serious problem. A raised temperature in a new baby usually indicates an infection of some kind. He may have caught a bacterial infection during birth or may have become infected with a cold virus from a visitor. Either way, a healthcare provider should always see a young baby with a suspected fever, as treatment may be required.

What's particularly important when your child has a fever is to make a note of his temperature each time you take it, so that you can keep track of any developments. Also, bear in mind that there are numerous things you can do to reduce your baby's high temperature before resorting to medicine. Look at his immediate environment and ask yourself: 'What is he wearing; can any of these clothes can be removed? Is the room too hot, and can I make it cooler? Is he lying on a thick blanket that reflects heat, and if so, can it be removed? Am I holding him so close that my own body heat is pushing up his temperature; shall I lay him down? When did he last have a cool drink; shall I give him some water?' These measures should help as his body struggles to fight off the infection.

Febrile convulsions

The normal body temperature is 37°C (98.6°F). If your child's temperature rises too far above normal (38.5°C [101.3°F]), this may result in febrile convulsions. Your child suddenly becomes rigid, stares without blinking, or his limbs start to twitch or jerk. He may become blue and lose consciousness for a few minutes. While frightening, febrile convulsions are quite common, especially in children between six months and three years of age, and are due to a child's temperature-lowering mechanism in the brain being too immature to cope.

To prevent a fever becoming convulsive, take your child's clothes off and sponge him down all over with tepid water. The evaporating water will help lower his temperature. Do not use cold water because this causes the blood vessels to contract and less heat will be lost.

Pat him dry and cover him lightly in a cotton sheet. Keep checking his temperature and add clothes gradually. If his temperature begins to rise again, repeat the sponging process or fan him. Offer him plenty of cool drinks.

Give your child paracetamol (12.5 mg/kg per dose) and ibuprofen (5 mg/kg per dose) alternatively, according to the packet instructions. This is more effective for lowering temperature or fever than giving only one of the medicines. Never give aspirin to a child under 12 unless directed

to do so by a doctor. If your child does develop convulsions, try not to panic. Keep sponging and make sure he is cool but not chilly. Move any objects that could be harmful out of the way and lie him down on his tummy or side, with his head turned to one side and tilted back slightly, so that the airway is clear. Remove any objects from your child's mouth. Do not put anything in the mouth. Stay with your child. Most fits will stop after three minutes. Reassure your child and call your doctor or an ambulance.

Meningitis

This is an inflammation of the membranes that line the brain and spinal cord. It's usually caused by a viral or bacterial infection. Viral meningitis may be caused by a number of different viruses, and is commonly mild, with no long-term side effects. Very occasionally it can be severe and cause serious problems.

With a newborn, bacterial meningitis is usually caused by Group B streptococcus. In babies over three months, the three most common forms of meningitis are: haemophilus influenzae Type B (Hib); meningococcus Groups A, B and C. Group B is the most common, but Group C is the most severe and requires immediate hospital treatment, as it can be fatal if not treated early.

If you suspect meningitis, call a doctor without delay or take your baby to the hospital for urgent evaluation. Meningitis may be hard

to diagnose, so your healthcare provider may perform a lumbar puncture to confirm any diagnosis. Antibiotics will be given if bacterial meningitis is suspected. A hearing test may be carried out after four weeks, as deafness is the most common side effect of bacterial meningitis. If the infection is viral, your baby should recover within a few days.

Earache

A pain in the ear may be caused by an infection in the middle ear (otitis media), by another infection such as measles or mumps, or by toothache. Symptoms include fever,

---

SIGNS OF MENINGITIS

- High-pitched crying
- Drowsiness or lethargy
- Bulging fontanelle (soft spot) on the top of a baby's head
- Vomiting
- Refusal to feed
- Pale skin and cold limbs
- Sensitivity to light
- Fever and a blank, staring expression
- Stiffness of the neck
- Difficulty breathing
- A convulsion with stiffened body and shaking
- Reddish-purple spots that don't go away if pressed with a glass and that develop into bruises under the skin

FIRST AID FOR CHOKING

Babies under a year old usually choke because they have breathed in a foreign object, which can lodge at the back of the throat and cause muscle spasm. This may block the airway and must be removed immediately. If you suspect your baby is choking but he can still cry and cough, allow him to continue coughing. Watch carefully but do not pat his back or give water.

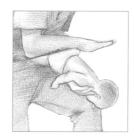

If he cannot cry, cough or breathe, or is making high-pitched noises, remove any obvious obstructions first but do not do sweep your fingers in his mouth. Lay him along your forearm on his tummy; rest your forearm on your upper thigh with your baby's head extending past your bent knee. With the heel of your other hand, strike your baby between the shoulder blades five times. Each strike should be a separate attempt to dislodge the object.

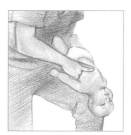

If your baby is still choking, carefully turn him over and place two or three fingers in the centre of his breastbone. Give five chest thrusts. Each thrust should be 1 to 2 cm (½ to 1 in) deep, and should be a separate attempt to dislodge the object. Check his mouth after each cycle of five thrusts. If the obstruction does not clear after three cycles of back blows and chest thrusts, dial 999 (or 112) for an ambulance. Continue as above until help arrives.

If your baby loses consciousness but is still breathing, place him on his back, tilting his head back slightly and, using a single finger, carefully feel and remove any obstruction from his mouth. If your baby remains unconscious and stops breathing, get help and start **CPR** (see page 124). If there is a pulse but no breathing, perform rescue breathing. To do this, gently tilt his head back with one hand, and lift his chin with the other to open his airway. Seal your lips over his mouth and nose and give one small breath every three seconds until he starts breathing on his own.

---

severe pain, general unwellness and vomiting. If the ear drum bursts, yellow or green pus or blood may be seen in the ear or on the pillow.

If your child has earache but is otherwise well, give paracetamol for 12–24 hours. Do not put any oil or eardrops into your child's ear. A covered hot water bottle or a heat pad can be placed under your child's ear to relieve pain. If your child appears to have an infection, consult your doctor. Your doctor may either prescribe antibiotics or recommend paracetamol and decongestant nose drops.

After an ear infection your child may have a hearing problem for up to six weeks. If this persists see your doctor for advice.

Diarrhoea
Usually caused by the rotovirus infection, diarrhoea is characterised by frequent, loose, watery, foul-smelling stools, which may contain mucus and may be brown, yellow or green. Young children may also get a condition called toddler diarrhoea where bouts of passing very loose stools, which may contain bits of undigested food, occur for no apparent reason.

(CPR) CARDIOPULMONARY RESUSCITATION FOR BABIES UNDER ONE YEAR

1 Lie your baby down on a firm flat surface such as the floor or a table, then gently tilt his head back with one hand, and lift his chin with the other to open his airway. It's important not to tilt his head back too far as this could kink his airway. Put your ear to his mouth and nose, and look, listen and feel for breathing.

2 If your baby is not breathing, give him five Rescue Breaths: Ensure the airway is open. Seal your lips around his mouth over his nose and lips. Blow gently into the lungs looking along the chest as you breathe. Fill your cheeks with air and use this amount each time. As the chest rises, stop blowing and allow it to fall. Repeat five times.

3 Then give 30 chest compressions: Place the baby on a firm surface. Locate a position in the centre of the chest and, using two fingers, press down sharply about one-third of the depth of the chest. Press 30 times at a rate of 100 per minute.

4 After 30 compressions, give two Rescue Breaths. Continue resuscitation (30 compressions to two Rescue Breaths) without stopping until help arrives.

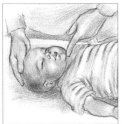  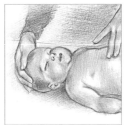 

If the diarrhoea is very watery or contains blood, it continues for more than 48 hours, your child is also vomiting, or has signs of dehydration (dry skin or mouth, sunken eyes, does not pass water for six to eight hours, or is listless), contact your doctor immediately.

To treat, give your child plenty of clear fluids or an oral electrolyte fluid. Let him continue to eat if he wants to but avoid too much milk or fruit.

Chickenpox

A common and mild viral infection, which most children have had by the age of 10, the virus is easily spread by airborne droplets. In rare cases it can lead to encephalitis.

Spots appear mainly in crops over three to four days. These change to blisters and crust over. Your child will have a slight fever and appears unwell and may have a headache.

To soothe the itching, apply calamine lotion, or give the child a tepid bath with a cup of bicarbonate of soda or oatmeal added. Discourage scratching as it can cause scarring. For a fever, give paracetamol and plenty to drink.

Never give aspirin as this can cause complications. Contact your doctor; your doctor may prescribe antiseptic cream.

Try to keep your child away from anyone who is pregnant as contacting chickenpox in pregnancy may cause serious problems for the mother and baby. If your child was with anyone pregnant just before he became unwell, tell the woman to see her doctor.

Fifth Disease

A fairly common but mild viral infection, usually occurring in the spring. The major symptom is a slap mark on cheek, which lasts one to two days. Over the next two to three days, a lacy red rash appears on the body. It may come and go for up to two weeks. There may be fever and nasal discharge.

Keep your child cool and give him plenty to drink. The child is not contagious once the rash appears so does not need to be kept away from others. The rash generally causes no discomfort and goes away eventually without treatment. There are no complications.

German measles (rubella)

This is a viral disease, which is usually mild in children but can be serious for adults, therefore it is best to be exposed to it as a child. Rubella can be prevented by immunisation.

It may start like a cold but spots appear on the face, and spread to the rest of the body. The rash usually only lasts for a few days. Your child will usually feel fine but he may have a slight fever and enlarged lymph nodes at the back of his neck on the lower part of the skull. Give him plenty to drink. Keep the child away from pregnant women – if a pregnant woman catches rubella during the first four months of pregnancy, there is a serious risk of damage to her baby.

Whooping cough

This is a very distressing disease and can be dangerous in young children but it can be prevented by immunisation. Complications can include pneumonia, convulsions, ear infections, brain damage and even death. Keep a child with whooping cough away from non-immunised babies.

Whooping cough starts with a cold and cough but the cough gradually gets worse and changes so that several bouts occur in succession. These are exhausting for your child who may find it difficult to breathe and may vomit or choke. The coughing usually, but not always, ends with a 'whoop' as the child gasps for breath. It may last for several weeks.

Call your doctor. Antibiotics will be needed, and in severe cases, hospitalisation. Keep your child cool. Give drinks and offer food immediately after a coughing bout. If your child is having a choking coughing fit, place him on your knee, lean him forward and gently pat and rub his back to help loosen the mucus.

Impetigo

This common bacterial skin infection in children usually occurs around the nose and mouth. It spreads rapidly, especially in warm weather. Complications can include swelling of lymph nodes, septicaemia or kidney inflammation.

Spots form blisters filled with yellow sticky fluid which oozes from the skin. The fluid dries to form honey-coloured crusts on the skin.

Consult your doctor immediately because impetigo spreads rapidly if left untreated. Topical antibiotics, covered by dressings, and sometimes oral antibiotics will be needed. Wash away crusted areas with warm water; pat dry with paper towels. Keep your child's flannel, towels and bedlinen separate from the rest of the family. Keep your child at home until he is fully recovered.

Infantile eczema

Also known as atopic dermatitis, this is the most common form of eczema in babies under 12 months. Eczema is an allergic condition related to asthma and hay fever. It can be inherited but also can exist in isolation. It commonly appears on the face and scalp or behind the ears. Your baby may only have a few patches of dry skin; but if the eczema is severe, your baby's skin may become sore, inflamed and weepy. This is unbearably itchy, so your baby will scratch continuously, leaving his skin open to infection.

Though it can only be managed, not cured, most children do grow out of atopic eczema. It is important to maintain a strict skin-care regime under medical supervision. Emollients will prevent your baby's skin from getting too dry and itchy. Steroid creams can reduce inflammation, but are generally only used if your baby's eczema hasn't responded to emollients. Antibiotics may be prescribed to clear up infection in severe cases.

Wearing mitts will help to stop a baby scratching. Breastfeeding for the first six months may give some protection against allergens.

Index

Acknowledgements

Products supplied by Mothercare.
All products available at
www.mothercare.com

Picture Credits

P 2/3 Camera Press/Eltern: P 7 Terry
Allen/Photolibrary Group: P 9
Camera Press/Eltern: P 12
Photolibrary Group: P 16,19, 21, 44
Getty Images: P 51 Camera
Press/Eltern: P 52 Getty Images
P 56 Camera Press/Richard
Stonehouse: P 57
www.bloomingmarvellous.co.uk:
P 58t, b, 68, 70, 82, 84, 87, 88t, 92/3
Getty Images: P 97 Camera
Press/Richard Stonehouse: P 102
Camera Press/Images 24: P 108
Camera Press/Richard Stonehouse:
P 113, 121 Getty Images
Front jacket Getty Images